A Woman for God's Glory

CHRISTIAN LIGHT PUBLICATIONS INC
P.O. BOX 1212
Harrisonburg, Virginia 22801-1212
(540) 434-0768

© 1990 Mrs. Bennie Byler
Endorsed by Calvary Publications, Kalona, Iowa

Distributed by Choice Books of Northern Virginia
11923 Lee Highway, Fairfax, VA 22030   (703) 830-2800

Copies may also be obtained from the author at:
Rt. 1, Box 630, Stuarts Draft, VA 24477

The author welcomes comments and letters.

ISBN: 0-940883-03-1

Attempt has been made to secure permission for the use of all copyrighted material. If further information is received, the publisher will be glad to properly credit this material in future printings.

PRINTED BY CAMPBELL COPY CENTER
Harrisonburg, Virginia

Endorsements

We are on a journey through life that the Bible likens to "a vapor that appeareth for a little time, and then vanisheth away." God has a purpose for each of us to fulfill.

God ordained the home and the church as major channels to carry on His work. Parents are called of God to direct their children to walk in righteousness and serve Him. Ministers and their wives have a specific calling to assist others in the ways of righteousness. This book is written to help Christian women become their best for God.

In this book you'll find help in developing godly attitudes to assist you along your journey. You'll find encouragement and direction for reaching out and helping others and also be reminded of the "inner beauty" that touches the lives of others, the joy of walking in obedience, and the reward of being righteous before God.

Being helpful comes out of a vibrant relationship with God and others. The spiritual success of a husband is very dependent on the loyalty and faithfulness of his companion.

A WOMAN FOR GOD'S GLORY is a helpful jewel. Read on—you will be enriched.

—Simon Schrock

Much is written about the role of women in society. Self-realization and fulfillment seem to be key words.

Anna Mary Byler and the other writers of this book believe that we cannot improve upon God's formula for happiness. They believe that the highest fulfillment is found in the center of God's will. It is written by people who view Christian womanhood as a sacred privilege, an exciting challenge. These authors have the credentials of personal experience. The book is a testimony of faith, obedience, and blessing. It is a record of God's faithfulness in a variety of real life experiences.

The book is commended to the reader for its value in promoting fulfillment and wholeness in a fragmented society. It will provide strength and encouragement in an area of urgent need.

—David L. Miller

A Woman
for
God's Glory

*"That we should be to
the praise of His glory . . ."*

Table of Contents

Writer's Acknowledgements

O Lord, our Lord, how excellent is thy name in all the earth!

Psalm 8:1

I am deeply indebted . . .

To my Heavenly Father for extending His mercy to me —counting me worthy to live "for His glory."

To my loving husband, Bennie, for reading my "scrawls" before the manuscripts were typed or read by anyone else. This book is in fact an extension of his ministry.

To my faithful children, Steve and Rosalind, Sue, Sharon, and Shirley, for their tireless encouragement, for typing and retyping, And especially for my three daughters, for designing the cover of the book.

To my "spiritual parents," Roman and Amanda Mullet, with whom I first shared my dream and concern. Especially to Amanda—who wrote three chapters and the Introduction—whose encouragement and prayers have been a great blessing.

To Ervin and Barbara Hershberger for giving unselfishly many days to read, reconstruct, proofread, and finally, type the final manuscript. Barbara also submitted some of the poems preceding the chapters. Without their help, this book would not have become a reality.

To the twelve willing wives who shared my concern and gave of themselves by sharing personal experiences and taking time to write.

To David L. and Paul Miller, Simon Schrock, and Elmer and Lovina Gingerich and Linda Rose Miller who spent hours reading and rereading the manuscript to correct flaws and errors.

To all of you readers who have a deep desire to truly become a "Woman for God's Glory." To you I trust this book will become a blessing.

To those at Pilgrim Fellowship who permitted me to use some experiences and those who encouraged, prayed, and helped with the typing.

I also acknowledge my humanity. I have meant to be fair, accurate, and truthful in all of my writing. In doing so, I am aware that I "hung out my wash for all to see," but I am deeply grateful for the blood of Jesus that cleanses, purifies, and covers. There is victory, and victory is available to all who are willing to pay the price of discipleship.

O Lord, our Lord, how excellent is thy name in all the earth!
Psalm 8:9

Introduction

by Amanda (Mrs. Roman) Mullet

Out of the heartbeat and concern of Anna Mary Byler (wife of Bennie Byler), and her insistent belief that God is a great God who answers prayers, this book was inspired and developed.

Bennie was born May 19, 1943, and Anna Mary (Yoder) Byler was born September 19, 1943. They were married March 19, 1964. They have four children: Susan Delores, Stephen Jay (married to Rosalind McGrath); Sharon Regina (married to Kenneth Troyer); and Shirley Ann. They also have two grandchildren: Douglas Adam and Margaret Lucinda.

Bennie was ordained deacon March 19, 1972, and to the office of bishop December 16, 1973, both at Pilgrim Fellowship, Stuarts Draft, Virginia.

Their flourishing business (constructing storage buildings) reflects the same diligence evidenced in the building of God's Kingdom. Alert to the needs of people around them, they give counsel, advice, and physical help wherever needed.

They have been a stabilizing factor in our lives, as well as in many others. Their love for the church and her functions is reflected in the timely subjects selected for this book. "The Minister's Wife and Her Responsibilities," "The Minister's Children," "The Missionaries Abroad," "Communications Between Husband and Wife," "Vacations," etc., are only a few of the many subjects covered.

As we read through these pages, let us shine a spotlight on the examples, illustrations, and encouragements, as well as on the things that may be found wanting in our own lives. By so doing not only we, but also the generations to come, may know the joy and power of triumphant manhood and womanhood through Jesus Christ.

By praying and clinging to God, believing and trusting in Him, these interests have become a part of Anna Mary's life. Her family has also been a real blessing in showing an interest and helping in this venture.

It is our mutual prayer that lives may be touched and enriched by this book. May God Himself be glorified and honored for all the efforts put forth in these writings.

Preface

by Ervin Hershberger

Woman is the glory of the man (I Cor. 11:7b). She is an help meet [suitable] for him (Gen. 2:18). She supplements and complements deficient areas of his make-up. A proper blending of masculine and feminine virtues and strengths is God's design for ultimate blessings to both.

Ministers particularly need the help and companionship of a good wife, especially when counseling sisters, or in dealing with matters pertaining to sisters. Only God knows how much of a minister's success is due to the loyal support and help of a faithful wife, both openly and behind the scenes! Her lack of support may result in her husband's failure—sometimes in disqualification.

Just as ministers need to consult and counsel with one another, so their wives are stimulated, encouraged and edified by communicating with one another concerning their roles as ministers' wives. That is primarily what this book is all about. One of these writers is not a minister's wife, but a mother with unique and challenging experiences worth sharing with anyone.

Ministers and laymen, brethren and sisters, young or old, married or single can benefit by reading this book. It should stimulate us to a life of service for the Lord, at home or abroad.

Relatively few brethren are ordained, and relatively few sisters are called to be ministers' wives, but every Christian is called to a life of service. Whatever your calling or station in life, you can be either *A Woman (or a man) to God's Glory.*

"I can do all things through
Christ
which strengtheneth me."
Philippians 4:13

Not Alone

"Be still and know that I am God,"
That I who made and gave thee life
Will lead thy faltering steps aright:
That I who see each sparrow's fall
Will hear and heed thy earnest call.
I am thy God.

"Be still and know that I am God,"
When aching burdens crush thy heart,
Then know I form thee for thy part
And purpose in the plan I hold.
Trust in Me.

"Be still and know that I am God."
Who made the atom's tiny span
And set it moving to My plan,
That I who guide the stars above
Will guide and keep thee in My love,
Be thou still.

—Author unknown

Apprehended By God

by Anna Mary (Mrs. Bennie) Byler

It was a beautiful, calm, cool night. The stars were shining so brightly, and the breeze was floating through the open window. One look into the dark, serene night would indicate that all was at rest and at peace. But it was not so in the heart of a young girl who looked out into the night, beyond the twinkling stars to the Creator of the universe, and cried as though her heart would break.

She was wondering for perhaps the hundredth time why God chose to bring deep sorrow to such a young and helpless family. Why would He leave the responsibility to raise four children plus care for a dairy farm? Why did God take their father, when, in their way of thinking, he was needed. Why? . . . when it seemed he was the one who held the family together, and now God chose to take him home and leave the family to struggle alone. Why? . . . when there were so many questions a young sixteen-year-old needed to have answered. Why? . . . when there was such a deep, empty, hurting feeling. Why? . . . when other families were complete and seemingly had few struggles. Why? Dear God, why?

In the stillness of the night, her cry was not heard by any mortal. Yet God was listening, and God heard; and, as always, God answered! Not until the sobbing subsided,

1

however, could she hear those kind, gentle words of her Heavenly Father, "I know you loved your father. I know all the sorrow, all the tears. Just put in Me all the trust and confidence that you had in your father. Rest in Me. I'll carry your family through this valley of sorrow. Trust Me; I'll be your Father." What consolation, what healing for a sorrowing heart, what comfort . . . and with that assurance, she fell asleep.

Now, thirty years later, God is still proving His faithfulness. He is still the loving heavenly Father, and He has carried the family through many trying times. He is still leading today in ways too wonderful for me to comprehend.

Don't ever be afraid to "be brought to a stop" by God. Don't be afraid to trust your life to the One Who "can take and keep our souls in His custody." Don't be afraid when you feel that hand of discipline on your life. It's our loving heavenly Father, Who in love has apprehended you for His own.

Ephesians chapter one emphasizes our purpose for living "to the praise of the glory of his grace" (v. 6) and: ". . . to the praise of his glory" (vv. 12, 14). It is our calling to bring glory to God by our service to our fellowmen and because of our adoration for our Saviour and Lord.

"Blessed is the [woman] that trusteth in the Lord, and whose hope the Lord is. For [she] shall be as a tree planted by the waters, and that spreadeth out her root by the river, and shall not see when heat cometh, but her leaf shall be green; and shall not be careful in the year of drought (or restraint), neither shall cease from yielding fruit" (Jeremiah 17;7, 8).

Do not be afraid to commit your life to your heavenly Father and use the abilities God has entrusted to you. In

Ephesians 4:7 He promises us, "But unto everyone of us is given grace according to the measure of the gift of Christ." "For ye are bought with a price: therefore glorify God in body, and in your spirit, which are God's" (I Cor. 6:20). It is only our reasonable service to be "A Woman for His Glory." God said, "I know thee by name, and thou hast also found grace in my sight" (Exodus 33:12b). "My presence shall go with thee, and I will give thee rest" (v. 14).

But with every promise there is a condition we must meet. We must be ready to hear God and to do His bidding. We must come to Him, which would mean we must separate ourselves from the cares and allurements of this world. We need to present ourselves to God to be of service to our families and those whom God has entrusted to our care.

God is a jealous God (Exodus 34:14). He deserves our utmost praise and adoration all the days of our life.

So with the consolation that God loves us and He wants all of our devotion, can we say with Jeremiah, ". . . as for me, I have not hastened from being a [pastor's wife] to follow Thee"?

"Too Busy"

The Lord had a job for me,
   but I had so much to do.
I said: "You get somebody else—
   or wait till I get through."
I don't know how the Lord made out,
   but He seemed to get along,
But I felt very guilty
   for I knew I'd done God wrong.

One day I needed the Lord,
   needed Him right away—
And He never answered me at all,
   but I could hear Him say
Down in my accusing heart—
   "Sorry, I've got too much to do.
You get somebody else
   or wait till I get through."

Now, when the Lord has a job for me,
   I never try to shirk;
I drop what I have on hand
   and do the good Lord's work;
And my affairs can run along,
   or wait till I get through.
Nobody else can do the work
   that God's marked out for you.

—Paul Lawrence Dunbar
—Adapted

Enrolled In The School Of Obedience

by Anna Mary (Mrs. Bennie) Byler

It was a beautiful tropical Belizean morning, as I was sitting by the window looking over the already busy countryside.

My morning devotions were from Isaiah chapter thirty. Verse twenty-one was a real challenge to me: "Thine ears shall hear a word behind thee saying, This is the way, walk ye in it . . ." With deep thanksgiving to my heavenly Father for the wonderful privilege of being one of His children, I proceeded to do the many tiresome tasks in the inconvenient kitchen. It was reassuring, too, to know that God had indeed led our family to Double Head Cabbage for six weeks, granting the missionary family a much-needed furlough to the States.

The past several weeks had already been very full and rewarding as we were helping with summer Bible school. Now we were in the last week, and it seemed it was taking the Bible school teachers longer to return than usual.

When they did come home their faces were solemn. A little six-year-old Belizean, Terry, decided to jump from the moving cart that was towed by the Land Rover. He had been told to stay sitting, but, on an impulse, he leaped off right in front of the wheel. Of course, the wheel went over his body before Bennie could stop the Land Rover. By all appearances he was not hurt seriously, but in order to take every precaution, they took him to the city hospital an hour's drive away. The X-rays showed internal injuries. The doctor assured us that with surgery all would be well—but all was not well. Less than four hours later, he died from internal bleeding.

Many frustrations followed. In the police station the next day, there were threats of a jail sentence for manslaughter. There were the sorrow and heartache of the mother and grandmother; the compassion of the natives as they stopped by to share their sympathy and to assure us we were not to blame; the anger of Terry's Canadian father; the wake, all night drinking and card games; singing by the Bible school teachers; the funeral service conducted by Bennie; and the simple burial in Granny's back yard. Yes, all this and knowing, "This is the way, walk ye in it!"

Little do we know what God has for each of His children as we enter this "School of Obedience," this life of commitment. But how very wonderful to know that God makes no mistakes a⌐d He is always right there to carry us through.

Isaiah 26:3 tells us to trust God and to keep our eyes and minds stayed on Him. It is only then that we can clearly follow the Lord in true obedience.

One of the greatest goals is to have an untroubled and uncluttered mind. This is only possible as our minds are stayed on God. Then the reward will be a wonderful *"Calm-plex!"* We will be able, even in the midst of frustration, to think clearly and calmly. We will be able to thank God for any situation.

"I delight to do thy will, O my God, yea, thy law is within my heart" (Psalm 40:8). Submission to God is vitally important if we are to walk in obedience to Him. To many of us this means being submissive in our own homes to our husbands.

It is quite impossible to be in submission in our homes until we are able to say, "Lord, I want to be submissive in everything. Teach me how to make it practical in my life." We need this step before we are able to readily leave all the consequences of complete obedience to God.

Paul was indeed a classical example for all of us to follow. He told his followers to follow him as he followed Christ. We must keep the Biblical traditions of obedience and submission to be able to pass them on to the following generations.

Our obedience is measured by how obedient we are in private. Biblical submission and obedience are unconditional. Greater intelligence, maturity and competence excuses no one; but rather intensifies our responsibility to man and our accountability to God. "For unto whomsoever much is given, of him shall be much required" (Luke 12:48).

C.H. Spurgeon adequately illustrated true obedience to God. "God will be honey to my mouth, music to my ears, heaven in my heart, and all in all to all my being."

Preacher F.B. Meyer wanted God's fullest blessing and offered this prayer: "Lord, I am willing to be made willing about everything!" Isn't this often where we fail as God's children? We want God's fullest blessings, but are not "willing to be made willing in everything." This should be the heartbeat of every minister's wife who is really serious about heeding God's call of obedience.

"This I say then, Walk in the Spirit, and ye shall not fulfill the lust of the flesh" (Galatians 5:16). In order to walk in the Spirit, we must be filled with the Spirit of God. God never pushes His Spirit on anyone. In order to be filled, we must first be empty of self. The more empty we are of self, the more God's Spirit can be there to fill us. His Spirit will also make us aware where we need to be "emptied" even more. Walking and living in the Spirit of God is the antidote for selfishness. Then if we are filled and walking in the Spirit, our lives will also be in tune to hear the still, quiet bidding of God. If we walk in God's Spirit, we will serve one another in love (Galatians 5:13b).

Pilate's wife must have been a woman of intuition. She pleaded with her husband to "have nothing to do with that just Man." She allowed her dream to speak to her and shared her concern with her husband. (Yet the crucifixion was God's plan.)

We as ministers' wives must have obedient hearts, sensitive to God's quiet probings and pleadings, and in quietness and meekness "wait upon Him." In given situations we must at times share with our husbands, for God's glory.

Isabella of Castille, queen of Spain, prayed, "I beg Thee, Lord, to hear the praying of Thy servant. Show forth Thy truth and manifest Thy will with Thy marvelous works. Give me wisdom and courage to move forward with Thy arm alone."

Living in obedience to what we know, diligently reading and living God's Holy Word, are other steps to true obedience and being in tune with God. Then, and then only, can we be truly obedient.

It is also very important to cultivate the art of thinking. Nothing is as easy as thinking, and nothing is as difficult as thinking well—God's thought and words—thinking and meditating on the good of others. Thinking is always dangerous unless it is under the direction of the Spirit of God. A person is not what he thinks he is: *he is what he thinks!*

Queen Esther's inner beauty as well as her outer beauty was known by all who knew her. Even so our lives as wives should display the inward beauty of a truly obedient heart to our Lord and Saviour, and then to our husbands and families.

Proverbs 31:10 mentions virtue, or excellence. That virtuous woman was so called because she had conviction, and conviction brings influence. For that reason, it is so important that we ministers' wives practice what God sees as excellence. That way our life can be one of conviction and influence, in true obedience to God and His calling for our life.

The qualities that are found in Proverbs 31 should not be thought of as a threat, but much rather as God's pattern of a fulfilled, joyous, and dedicated woman whose goal is to be for God's glory. Note the following guidelines;

1. She is loyal to her husband. (10-12)
2. She is faithful in her home. (13-16)
3. She is tireless in her responsibilities. (17-19)
4. She is generous toward the needy. (20)
5. She is fearless about circumstances. (21-23)
6. She is honest in business matters. (24)
7. She is prepared for the future. (25)
8. She is wise in her utterances. (26)
9. She is dependable in daily duties. (27)
10. She is praised by her children. (28-29)
11. She is beautiful in her conduct. (30)
12. She is appreciated by her neighbors. (31)

If we love to follow God's Word in true obedience, then each of us can be "a crown to her husband" (Proverbs 12:4), and "to the praise of His glory" (Ephesians 1:12).

A woman is radiant in her later years
if she has used time wisely while young.
She has found . . . time to work—the price of success.
time to think—the sovereign power.
time to read—foundation of knowledge.
time to pray—the way of serenity.
time to think of others—the road to joy.
time to laugh—music of the soul.
time to rejoice—in the goodness of God.
time to light the flame—of sympathy and
tenderness.

Submitted by A.M.B.

Faithfulness Begins In The Heart

by Anna Mary (Mrs. Bennie) Byler

Zacharias and Elizabeth are examples of true faithfulness. We read the account in Luke where Zacharias was a priest and they both had a good testimony before God. "They were both righteous before God, walking in all the commandments and ordinances of the Lord blameless" (Luke 1:6). Two outstanding characteristics that they both possessed were "righteous before God," and "walked in all obedience." That is the best description one could have of true faithfulness.

What a beautiful picture—husband and wife both having this testimony. The challenge is ours today. God is still looking for faithfulness, and how sad—it is nearly a word of the past.

Faithfulness according to Webster would indicate loyalty, a way of life, and living with confidence.

In the twentieth century this is still God's way. He is still looking for the faithful, those who are righteous before Him and those who dare to obey all the commandments and ordinances of the Lord, blamelessly.

I am personally very thankful to our heavenly Father for the privilege of being blameless, or in other words, confessed up to date. Many are the times Satan tries to undermine God's plan and will in my life. Yet when I realize

11

I have erred, I can confess my sins (we would rather call them faults) and again be in right standing before God.

Seemingly there is a trend today: "What one doesn't know, won't hurt him." But be not deceived, God is not mocked. It does matter! After all, it is the heart that God sees and judges, and not the mask that one wears.

Faithfulness in the heart was described by someone as "being the same skin, but a new person within."

"Blessed are the pure in heart, for they shall see God [in everything]" (Matthew 5:8). A pure heart is a must if one is to be faithful. "Let your light so shine before men, that they may see your good works and glorify your Father which is in heaven" (Matthew 5:16). There needs to be conviction in our hearts if we are faithful. Conviction is noted by one writer as hands and feet of our commitment to God.

Daniel is one example of faithfulness. "But Daniel purposed in his heart that he would not defile himself . . ." (Daniel 1:8). In this account we notice that God blesses faithfulness. Probably if Daniel would not have purposed in his heart, God could not have used him in such a marvelous way. If there was ever a time in history that this was needful, it is needful today. It will be largely determined by our faithfulness to God in the hidden recesses of our heart.

The challenge to us mothers is to be a living example of God's purposes. We need to live what we say. Our children know us better by what we are than by what we say. We need to be a true reflection of God.

Our faithfulness to God determines what our children will become. If we practice what we say, we will be conveying to our children the importance of faithfulness; therefore, we will develop a God-consciousness early in their lives.

Hannah was a good example of a mother who dedicated her son before he was born and in 1 Samuel 2:26 we read the result. "He grew . . . in favor with both the Lord, and also with men." We must hold forth the word of life by living God's Word and making it our life.

Andrew Murray is yet another example of faithfulness that paid dividends. Of Murray's eleven children five sons became ministers and four daughters became ministers' wives. In his next generation, the record is is still more striking. Ten grandsons became ministers and thirteen became missionaries. What greater rewards for faithfulness are there than that of knowing God works through generations to come? Perhaps many of us will not live to see generations to come, yet as we seek to live the Word of God, He promises to reward faithfulness in generations to come.

Faithfulness in the heart is an inner beauty. "It is the divinity within that makes the divinity without."

We must have true heart-beauty if we are going to teach our children to be faithful in the little unnoticed areas of life. The challenge is ours. Are we really living the fullest and finest for Him?

A Quaker woman's recipe for beauty was described by the following: "Truth—the use of the lips; Prayer—the use for the voice; Sympathy—the use for the eyes; Service—the use for the hands; Uprightness—the use for the figure; and Charity—the use for the heart."

If we are faithful at heart we will demonstrate the fruits of the Spirit. "An affectionate, lovable disposition, radiant spirit and cheerful temper, a tranquil mind and quiet manner, a forbearing patience in provoking circumstances with trying people, a sympathetic insight and tactful helpfulness, generous judgment, loyalty and reliability under all circumstances, humility that forgets self in the joy of helping others. In all things self-mastery and self-control which is the final work of perfection."[1]

Meekness is another characteristic that we need in order to be faithful. It is the inner strength that comes to us when we lay down our will to accomplish God's will. Meekness is also defined as the power of God in practice. A meek person accepts God's dealings without murmurings, complainings, or resistance. Always accept God as good and all-wise.

"Humility is perfect quietness of heart. It is for me to have no trouble, never to be fretted or vexed or sore, irritated or disappointed. It is to be at rest when no one praises me, or when I am blamed or despised. It is to have a 'blessed home in the Lord' where I am at peace as in a deep sea of calmness, when all around is trouble" (Selected, source unknown).

Discipline, too, is needed in the faithful heart. "For whom the Lord loveth he chasteneth, and scourgeth every son whom he receiveth" (Hebrews 12:6). Is this the way we view discipline, or do we complain and murmur? Do we see that God loves us? If not, then our own attitude will not be effective as we discipline our children, but rather we will instill in them the wrong concept of God and His love for us.

Wisdom cannot grow without discipline! When God disciplines His children, He enlarges their capacity to endure and bear fruit for His glory. We as mothers must keep this in mind as we discipline our children. They need to sense that we have their eternal good in mind.

There is a difference between discipline and punish-

1. *Spirit Fruit,* by John Drescher, Herald Press, Scottdale, Penna., 1974.

ment. Discipline is the deliberate stress we introduce into our children's lives to stretch their capacities for performance. Punishment is the painful consequences which result from misdeeds and violations to family standards or principles.

Someone made the interesting observation about Proverbs 22:6, noting three types of training. Perhaps this is where we parents fail to really develop faithfulness in the hearts of our children.

1. *"Dictatorial*—meaning arrogantly domineering, overbearing. *Strain* up a child in the way he shall go and just as soon as he is old enough he will depart from it and from you.

2. *"Permissive*—failing to enforce, tolerant. *Refrain* not a child in any way he desires to go and when he is old enough to be a man he'll still be a child.

3. *"Rational*—being understanding and reasonable. '*Train* up a child in the way he should go: and when he is old, he will not depart from it' (Proverbs 22:6).

"Train, strain, or never *refrain!* The choice is ours—the results are up to our children."[2]

Let us take the responsibility seriously to be truly faithful at heart, and that will instill this faithfulness into the hearts of our children. Be aware that the child's first and strongest source of inspiration and encouragment is his parents. And no one—child, youth, or adult—ever outgrows the need of loving and caring parents. Everyone desires to be loved, not only for what we do, but for who we are!

Something in the Christian home that can be worse

2. *Delightful Discipline,* by Louis Goodgame, Mott Media, Milfrod, Mich., 1977.

than having laws or rules is to have guidelines and not enforce them.

The atmosphere of the home has a great impact on our children, either for good or ill. I'm sure we all desire the best for our children and yet the human tendencies prevail so often.

"Thou shalt teach them diligently unto thy children, and shalt talk of them when thou sittest in thine house, and when thou walkest by the way, and when thou liest down, and when thou risest up. And thou shalt bind them for a sign upon thine hand, and they shall be as frontlets between thine eyes. And thou shalt write them upon the post of thy house, and on thy gates" (Deuteronomy 6:7-9). In verse 12 we are reminded, *"Beware lest thou forget the Lord!"* There is never a vacation from sharing with and teaching our children. God demands faithfulness on our part as parents if we are to have faithful children.

At a young age it is important that we fill our children's minds with Bible stories, character building stories, Scripture verses, and songs or hymns. Our own practice of learning and memorizing God's Word will be the strongest encouragement to our children to memorize Scripture.

In the tender years of life we are molding our children's lives. What do the mottoes on the walls of our homes display? Decorating our children's rooms with noble plaques, Bible verses and posters will instill a God-consciousness.

A mother bought a plaque for her son's sixteenth birthday that said, "Jesus, Saviour pilot me." Jesus and a young man were facing the wild together—Jesus at the helm, pointing the way. Another impressive point was the clouds. One was shaped like a lion's mouth (the world) open and ready to devour. Pointing this out and hanging it where the young teenager could see it, helped avoid other temptations that could have been hazardous for his young life.

Placing posters in strategic spots can also be thought-provoking. Such as "The will of God is nothing less, nothing else, nothing more. God always gives the best to those who leave the choice to Him." This was placed in a family van where it was in full view, and as the children grew up it made an indelible impact on their minds. Another good one is, "I have no greater joy than to hear that my children walk in truth" (III John 4).

The meaning of children's names can also be impressive. Find a piece of wood and glue on it a poster with the child's name and its meaning, then seal it with decoupage. This hung on a wall of the home can be encouraging to a child, and it also portrays the value of the child to his parents.

Pictures on lunch boxes have made an impression on our children. We are also aware that since many newspapers and magazines are filled with filth, magazines should be carefully chosen. Our libraries are important, and we need to choose carefully what we place there. Encyclopedias and Childcraft are educational, but they should be placed in the family room and read there. Then at one glance the parents can see what the study is about.

We do well to encourage our children to read, but their reading should take place in the family room, or around the dining room or kitchen table with the rest of the family. Reading behind locked doors should be prohibited. If in their early years this is practiced and maintained, it will not become a problem later.

Consider this: If JESUS doesn't have our children, SATAN does! There is no alternative!

Satan "as a roaring lion, walketh about, seeking whom he may devour" (I Peter 5:8). If a lion were within our homes or on our lawns, we would not sit around half asleep; we would be frenzied! God tells us to be sober (life is serious), be vigilant (be on guard), because the enemy is out to destroy.

So it is important to teach our children while they are young, and continue to be consistent as they grow older. We must take time to teach and train while we work, while we sit together around the table at mealtimes, while we travel on the highways. If we are truly sober and vigilant, we will take notice of the need of teaching because the time is short; Satan is real; and our goal is to instill faithfulness in the hearts of our children.

Yes, mothers, we are reflections; whether we are of God or not, whether we are true or false. Our lives are speaking of faithfulness or unfaithfulness.

We can be faithful and live above reproach *if* we are constantly doing God's commandments and judgments (1 Chronicles 28:7). "Serve Him with a perfect heart and with a willing mind: for the Lord searcheth *all* hearts, and understandeth *all* the imaginations of the thoughts: *if* thou seek Him, He will be found of thee: . . ." (v. 9).

When you have
　　nothing left but God,
you begin to learn
　　that God is enough.

A Blessed Life

Our lives can be a blessing—
   In the vineyard of the Lord,
As we're yielded to God's Spirit
   And obedient to His Word.

Our lives can be a blessing—
   To the Church—the chosen Bride,
As we love and help each other
   And walk closely side by side.

Our lives can be a blessing—
   To our friends and those we meet,
As we're filled with His sweet presence
   When we kneel at Jesus' feet.

Our lives can be a blessing—
   As we fill a Mother's role,
And our labors are more fruitful
   When Christ Jesus has control.

Our lives can be a blessing—
   To our Husbands every day,
When we faithfully support them
   As they study, work and pray.

Lord, make our lives a blessing—
   And keep us close to you
For only as we're blest by You
   Our lives will be a blessing, too!

by Martha (Mrs. David) King

The Blessing And Protection Of The Headship Veiling

by Anna Mary (Mrs. Bennie) Byler

P salm 91 expresses the happy state of the godly. Psalm 17:8, "Keep me as the apple of the eye, hide me under the shadow of thy wings."

Have you ever wondered if it is needful to wear a symbol of submission on your head? Have you been tempted to doubt the power of the headship veiling?

Is it worth all the trouble to brush, comb, shampoo, properly care for and keep your long hair in a godly, Christian manner?

These and many other questions may at times pop into our minds at unguarded moments. But we must always be ready to defend this all-important doctrine and guard it with jealous care, lest Satan is allowed to inject another thought into our minds about the significance of the veiling.

I Cor. 11:10 tell us, ". . . for this cause ought the woman to have power on her head, because of the angels." Angels understand the symbolism of the veiling, and who among us would desire to be without heaven's protection?

"But ye are come unto Mount Zion, and unto the city of the living God, the heavenly Jerusalem, and to an innumerable company of angels" (Heb. 12:22). Who of us as God's children does not want to be counted among those who are surrounded by such a company of angels? Who of us is powerful enough to withstand Satan without accepting God's order for our lives, and the provision our Heavenly Father has made for the protection and well-being of us women? God has provided an innumerable company of angels, ". . . and the number of them was ten thousand times ten thousand, and thousands of thousands . . ." (Rev. 5:11b). If we expect to be among the innumerable company that is around the throne worshipping our Lord and Saviour and saying, "Worthy is the Lamb that was slain, to receive power, riches, wisdom, strength, honor, glory, and blessing," we must be willing now to be counted among the minority!

God gives His angels charge over us to keep us in all our ways, as we walk in obedience to His Word (Psalm 91:11).

Throughout the Bible, promises are followed by a necessary condition on our part. So also as we live a life of submission to our Head, the Lord Jesus, and those in authority over us, we can claim the protection that God so desires to give to us as His children.

Here is a quote from the pamphlet, "Why Christian Women Wear the Headship Veiling" (Rod & Staff, Crockett, Ky.): "God has chosen to employ a visible means to keep us aware of the divinely-appointed man-to-woman headship arrangement. The divinely-supplied witness is that the woman is to have long, uncut hair. I Corinthians 11:6 states plainly that it is a shame for a woman to be shorn or shaven. Long, uncut hair is a glory to the woman. Because every Christian woman wants to be in daily communion with God, she keeps her head covered as a visible witness that she is prepared to pray at all times" (I Thess. 5:17, I Cor. 11:5).

From *The Christian Woman's Head Veiling,* by Richard C. Detweiler (Herald Press, Scottdale, Pa., 1959): "The head-covering is a voluntary veiling of her glory to give sign of her dedication to God's order."

In a message some years ago, a statement was made that has challenged me many times: "We Christian women may choose to wear veilings the size of bushel baskets, and still not experience the blessing and protection of the holy angels. It is only as we are really submitting ourselves to the Headship order, that we find real joy and peace in our lives."

All of us have read stories of how Christian women were protected by unseen (and sometimes seen) heavenly beings, and these stories grip our hearts. However, experiences that have become a part of oneself leave an indelible impression on our lives. Frequently it is in those times when conviction is born, God's Word becomes more precious, and the holy angels become very meaningful. I would like to share such a personal experience.

The morning dawned clear and bright, with promise of being a beautiful day. When Bennie and I headed for the Miami airport, I was eagerly looking forward to returning home to our family after having been gone nearly three weeks.

We had decided that there our ways would part—I would return home, and Bennie would continue on to Paraguay to complete the 1987 Delegation Trip with the Mission Board.

Knowing it was God's will for me to return to our family and for Bennie to continue a week longer, we approached the service desk—to discover that while we were enjoying 76-degree weather, our home community was experiencing a real winter blizzard! The temperatures were below zero; there were icy roads, deep drifts, and over 24 inches of snow, with more snow predicted!

With these reports, of course it was not safe to attempt the flight . . . . After waiting for several hours, though, the agent announced that the runways had been cleared and take-off had been approved.

This was my first experience in traveling alone by aircraft, and therefore I was a bit apprehensive. However, I was especially grateful to my heavenly Father for the promise that he never leaves us alone. With that confidence, I waved to my husband and boarded the plane.

All went well, and it was with a grateful heart that I saw the city of Baltimore come to view. After we landed, I quickly made my way to the service desk to confirm my last flight and was assured that the runways were still open. Again I thanked God silently for the wonderful way He cares for us. I found a chair where I relaxed, eagerly awaiting the call to board. Time moved slowly. I busied myself with a book, but only half concentrated on it, as I felt a bit uneasy. After waiting two hours I again went to the service desk and was told the flight was still on schedule.

Only minutes later, the loudspeaker brought to me the realization that no more flights would be leaving until the next morning, fifteen hours later!

My first impulse was "Lord, what shall I do?" How wonderful to call upon the Lord when He has promised to answer. Our heavenly Father never leaves nor forsakes His children. Just then I developed a deeper appreciation for the headship veiling, the protection of the angels and the symbol of God and man, whom I am subject to. With that consolation, I made my way to the service counter once more.

As I approached the desk, I was surrounded by a

number of people, but there were only four businessmen who were also scheduled to leave for our small country airport.

What were the alternatives? What was I going to do? The service lady seemed very unconcerned, but mentioned three options: first, I could stay right here in the lobby, which seemed so dingy on such a cold, bleak winter evening. The place would be deserted because no planes would be landing or taking off. Then there was the option of finding a motel room and spending the night, or renting a car and traveling the 200 miles with the four business- men.

At this point I called our children. After hearing my predicament they assured me of their prayers, and encour- aged me to travel to the airport town 30 miles from home.

The spokesman for the businessmen was Dr. Stickley. He talked to my son Steve and assured the children they would do their best to provide a safe trip home.

After each of the men had shaken my hand, Dr. Stickley said, "You pray, and we'll drive!" What a consolation to know here again that God had provided an outward symbol for a woman in God's order. Many fears went through my mind, but just knowing I was in God's care was sufficient!

The four-hour drive to Dr. Stickley's home proved to be interesting. The doctor talked about his family (a blessing). The second businessman told about his work as an engineer at the Walker Muffler Co., in Harrisonburg, Virginia. He had recently been transferred from a company in Montana. The other two young men had never seen snow, being from Guatamala. They were staying within seven miles of our home, so I offered that they could travel the last 30 miles with our family. They were so grateful to be able to reach their destination in time for their morning appointment.

The four men had never known about Mennonites, and I was privileged to share my testimony. I also shared about our delegation trip and our busy life as a minister's family.

I was blessed and challenged to meet Mrs. Stickley, who had coffee and chocolate pie awaiting us. Her gracious hospitality was a real challenge to me.

Some say this was a mere coincidence, but to me it was the hand of God, His blessing, and the blessed protection of His angels.

Mothers, what is your conviction? It will show up in your girls. Perhaps this is why we see the diminishing of the veiling little by little! The challenge remains. Is it important to us that we are responsible to teach and allow God to strengthen our convictions for the headship veiling?

As we teach our little daughters the importance of prayer, we should also teach them about the prayer veiling. It is not a one-time teaching experience, but we teach by example, precept upon precept, line upon line, here a little and there a little (Isa. 28:13).

Especially as they come to the age of accountability and accept Jesus as Saviour and Lord, the veiling should become more precious to them.

As we mothers share experiences from our private devotions, we will be encouraging them by example. We should also allow them time for their devotions. Perhaps at times we could ask where they are reading, and ask questions to encourage a deeper study as they grow older.

There are times when our daughters are placed in environments that are less than ideal. Therefore we need to commit them into the hands of the Lord and the protection of the angels. It is extremely important that they develop a personal relationship with the Lord. The depth of their relationship will be the deciding factor in how they respond to the evils around them.

Let me relate another experience our family faced. Less than two years ago our 17-year-old daughter worked in several homes in the community.

One day, after a normal morning of family devotions and breakfast together, plus her private devotions, she left for a day of house cleaning.

The Smith family consisted of parents, both teachers, and their three school-aged children.

As the morning wore on, she answered a knock at the front door. A man who identified himself as a propane gas repairman asked if he could check their kitchen range. Sharon told him that the Smiths had a electric range, but he didn't take her word for an answer. So she locked the door and checked. Of course, it was electric!

He still wasn't satisfied and asked if he could make sure, to which she obediently opened the door and led him to the kitchen. As soon as he had seen the stove, she backed toward the front door. As he followed, he made several critical remarks about the money the Smith family had. He said he was a close friend of theirs. To this Sharon made no comment.

She opened the door and he left, so she proceeded with her work. That evening she told us about the day and felt so weak and shaky, she had to sit down. Such fear gripped her that she refused to go back alone without taking someone else along (sometimes it was only a child).

Sharon related this experience to the Smiths, and they had no idea who the man could have been. Mr. Smith made the remark, "This man could have taken all our possessions, but he had better not touch you!"

We will never know all the intentions of this man, and yet we are persuaded that God kept Sharon safe. She was blessed by her close relationship with the Lord, her modest dress, and the headship veiling. To a 17-year-old, the incident made an indelible impression on her life and deepened her conviction for the headship veiling.

> You tell on yourself by the friends you seek,
> By the very manner in which you speak,
> By the way in which you employ your time,
> By the use you make of the dollar and dime.
> You tell what you are by the clothes you wear,
> By the spirit in which you burdens bear,
> By the kinds of things at which you laugh,
> By the records you play on the phonograph.
> You tell what you are by the way you walk,
> By the things of which you delight to talk,
> By the manner in which you bear defeat,
> By so simple a thing as how you eat,
> By the books you choose from a well-filled shelf;
> In these ways, and more, you tell on yourself.
> So there's really no particle of sense
> In an effort to keep up a false pretense.
>
> —Author Unknown

Blueprint for God's blessing:

1. Give God the first of every day.
2. Give God the first day of every week.

3. Give God the first of your income.
4. Give God the first consideration in every decision.
5. Give God's Son first place in your heart.

—Author Unknown

The Headship Veiling:
A Man's Point of View

The Christian woman's veil was always of great importance to me. As a young husband and father I was concerned that my wife would not miss out on the blessings of the veiling. I wanted her veil to be large enough and properly worn so she could maintain a proper relationship with the Lord. I knew it was there for the angels and I didn't want her to miss out on those blessings either. It had never occurred to me that the veil was to be of great importance to me as a husband and father, until the Lord opened my eyes.

It was one morning as my wife was busy in the kitchen and while our children were enjoying the morning with us that God helped me to realize that my wife could not even see her own veil. That morning it dawned on me for the first time that I was the one who could see it clearly. It was there as a symbol to me, to speak to me, and to cry out the message that God wants every man to hear. The message in I Cor. 11:1-16 became more real to me.

As I looked upon my wife's veil it began speaking to me in a silent, yet loud and clear voice, saying, "Gene, I believe in God's great headship order and am willing to give myself under your care and direction. I want you to guide me through life. I want to fully submit." Nearby stood my two innocent daughters. Their veils seemed to also cry out saying, "Daddy, we too believe God's chain of command and we want you to guide our home and direct our lives as we journey through life. We too are submitted to you."

I looked over at our boys (no veils), yet the Lord continued to speak to me. My boys were born to be leaders, and they were looking to me to bring them up so they would be prepared to be the leaders God intended them to be.

As this message flowed from the veiling, it reminded me of my awesome responsibility. Without saying a word, I fled to my room to fall on my knees before my Head, Jesus Christ. After spending some time with my Lord I was prepared to face the task before me and to pledge my support in guiding my family safely through. What a blessing that God has given us this ordinance. May we learn to appeciate the veil and as husbands and fathers respond properly. May our families enjoy the guidance and protection that God intended for them.

(Excerpt from a message on the headship veiling, preached by Eugene Eicher, from Grabill, Indiana)

Children
are like wet
cement—
whatever falls on them
makes an impression.

Mother Ponders

She groans with dismay at the dirty tracks on her clean floor, and the pile of greasy clothes to be washed again . . . , til she heard a widow sigh, "What a privilege to have a loving husband to wash for and clean up after!"

Her lively child was driving her to frustration and she sputtered, "He's into everything!" Then she saw the wistful look on the face of a retarded child's Mother and heard her say, "How I wish my little one could run and play like others!"

The clock seemed to race along. No sooner were the breakfast dishes cleared away then she had to think of preparing dinner. But then a single sister shared her struggle, "It's hard to cook for only one. Cooking for a family would be much more worth while and such a challenge!"

Mother's work is never done. There are always things that await her attention, cleaning, sewing, cooking. But a friend encouraged softly, "You are blessed to have your hands filled. Our childless home stays clean, but feels empty."

Her minister husband was called away, again. She was tempted to murmur, "It's not fair!" Then her neighbor, the wife of a drunkard, said lovingly, "I wish my husband were doing something worth while."

All the while her heavenly Father was watching. Gently told her, "You haven't come to this place by accident. This is the place, the very place I meant for you to fill; "MY GRACE IS SUFFICIENT!"

by Lavina Gingerich

The Gift Of Motherhood

by Anna Mary (Mrs. Bennie) Byler

The conversation between a mother and her two-year-old son went something like this: "Mama, when I grow up, I want to be a mama, like you!" What a compliment—how commendable!

In the book of Genesis and on down through the ages, motherhood has been part of God's divine plan. In God's sight it is a precious gift He has entrusted to woman. It is high on His list of priorities.

A mother's position is extremely significant in helping to make her family what it ought to be. It demands a total life involvement.

As we seek to fulfill this responsibility day by day, we get weary—physically weary, emotionally weary—sometimes ready to give up.

There may be times when the role of motherhood seems overwhelming, but then I need to recall the price of my redemption and compare how little I am giving of myself to those precious lambs of His fold. At that moment I am enabled to give up self-pity and, with new strength, continue my next duty.

Because of the great importance of the family and the effect it will have upon your child, I challenge you: "Are you willing to live your very life for that family?" A successful family will cost just that. Are you willing, especially while your children are growing up, to freely give up other activities—even good activities? To carefully tend the precious children God has committed to your charge, such sacrifice may be necessary, allowing you to concentrate on the tremendous privilege and responsibility to which God has called you. This is the significant position of motherhood!

A good thought to keep in mind is that we must consider not just what the child is today, but the possibilities of what he will become tomorrow.

Our children get their first impression of God from their parents. Our concept of God is revealed by how we face daily tasks and duties, also the unforeseen. By our attitude we are either giving the children a picture of God as understanding and compassionate, or as "holding the stick over our heads." If we have a good relationship with our heavenly Father, our attitudes will be of a kind and considerate nature; not permissive, but consistent. Then we will have a godly home, where peace and contentment reign. How can we expect to prepare our children to become well-adjusted adults when there is havoc and chaos at home?

A cheerful, joyous mother sets the stage of the home. When a child grows up in such an environment, he will be prepared to face a hostile world. It is our privilege to impersonate God's positive approach and therefore convey it to our children.

Early in life we must teach them to lie still when their diaper is being changed and to hold still when they are being dressed. Never play a game and let them fight!

When they are called, they need to come the first time they hear. Don't let your children say "No" to authority. It is our responsibility to teach them. We should be quick to reward them by showing appreciation for a job well done or for good behavior.

If parents fail to give encouragement and show appreciation, the children will seek approval elsewhere; and usually it's not the companionship appreciated by their parents. Do we know our children's friends? We need to be alert to outside influences, bad company, clubs, etc. Our homes and churches should be providing all our children need to guide them on the path to heaven.

If we as parents expect to have our children's attention and respect when they are grown, we need to respect them now. There are no "busy signals" in the home of effective parents. We will have time to be interested in their interests.

It was a hurried Sunday morning when a little three-year-old son came running to the bathroom where his Daddy was shaving. Excitedly he exclaimed, "Daddy, come quick! There are deer in the pasture!"

Daddy looked at his watch and the shaving-creamed face and said, "Gary, just wait a minute," and proceeded to finish his shave.

When at last Daddy was finished, he looked for the deer, and, of course, the deer had been scared away. How much better to have just gone to the window and looked at the deer. Gary would have long remembered that Sunday morning when Daddy, with his well-lathered face, took time to look at the deer with him.

True love is proven when you happily listen to your child. Though sound asleep, you wake to your baby's faintest cry. You listen to the baby. Listen also when he is older. Any boy or girl needs to know their mother is interested and willing to listen to what they say. To them it says, "I value you—you are important to me!" God always has time to listen to His child, and we dare not disappoint our child by being too busy to listen.

Don't say, "Go play," when your child wants your attention, but rather listen and give time to your children. You will be richly repaid.

Appreciation is an attitude that is caught. The mother teaches by words, but attitudes are caught, more than taught.

When the child is a baby, and he has discomforts, we as mothers are quick to show comfort and care. This same love and compassion must go right on to preschool children, the adolescent, the teenager, and as long as they are part of our family. Never should we as parents make light of their problems. This cuts deeply into the child's heart. His troubles are as big as his capacity to face them, and the least we can do is listen and be understanding. Remember, we too, were once in that stage. We are wise if we remind ourselves how it felt.

In II Kings 20:1 God told King Hezekiah through a prophet, "Set thine house in order." That has been said centuries ago, but God's Word still stands. If we mothers want God's blessing in our homes, we must daily set our house in order. I am sure women's temperaments vary, and God has created us differently, but the statement is still in God's Word. He expects us to have an orderly home where our children can grow up and live an orderly life. Effective family life does not just happen. It's the result of deliberate, intentional determination and practice.

If we are really in earnest about being effective mothers, there are three words of which we must have a good understanding. *Wisdom* is the ability to discern; to view life as God sees it. *Understanding* is the skill to respond with insight. *Knowledge* is the trait of learning with prudence and discovering growth.

Isaiah 11:2 is describing Jesus: "And the Spirit of the Lord shall rest upon him, the Spirit of *wisdom* and *understanding*, the spirit of counsel and might, the spirit of *knowledge* and of the fear of the Lord." All that we need to be an effective mother is found in this verse, and what a wonderful privilege to have Jesus reside in our hearts. Then we will be effective mothers who by God's grace will start early in training, being balanced and consistent.

So why despair? God is always the same. "Jesus Christ the same yesterday, and today, and forever" (Heb. 13:8).

The secret is in total dedication—reserving nothing for self! "I beg you, therefore, Mothers, by the mercies of God that you present your lives and bodies a living sacrifice [offering to God something precious], holy, acceptable unto God, that is only our reasonable service" (Romans 12:1, paraphrased).

If we really are serious about our role of motherhood, God is always there to receive the dedication we give to Him. It is never too late to re-evaluate our lives, cleanse those hidden recesses of our hearts, and give Jesus full control of our hearts and lives. If we do this, God has wonderful blessings in store for us.

"Bring the *whole tithe*" (includes everything—our lives, our children, our all). "Test me in this," says the Lord Almighty, "and see if I will not throw open the flood gates of heaven and pour out so much blessing that you will not have room enough for it" (Malachi 3:10, NIV). This has been my experience. We can never outgive God. The more dedicated our lives are, the richer His blessings are.

A number of Bible women of outstanding character are a challenge to us as mothers.

Lois and Eunice are examples of a godly mother and grandmother. Their lives were invested in fervent prayer and unfeigned faith (II Timothy 1:5). The hidden blessings of praying without ceasing (I Thess. 5:17) are perhaps the most important in the life of an effective mother. As we are caring for our children during the night when everyone else is sleeping, Satan is there with frustrations and fears of the future, but God is also there. Developing the spirit of prayer when these fears enter our minds, will enable us to better face the next day. It also strengthens our faith, and how needful it is to be mothers of faith! A faithful mother takes God at His Word, and lives His Word to the fullest. Prayer has much to do with our children's future and success.

Deborah is called a mother in Israel. She was a strong woman, having unswerving faith and clear insights from God (Judges 5:7). God is today still looking for mothers like that!

Hannah's prayers helped Samuel through many trials and hard times. Samuel was an outstanding judge in Israel for many years. If we are women of prayer, we will also be women of purpose.

Mary, John Mark's mother, was a widow and a woman of prayer. The disciples met at her house (Acts 12), and when Peter was released he knew where to find them. Miracles still take place when mothers pray. John Mark became a writer and wrote the Gospel of Mark.

Salome ministered to Jesus' needs and came to Jesus with a request for her sons. We need to be more concerned that our children find God's will for their lives than to desire our children to be "in the limelight."

Elizabeth, the mother of John the Baptist, the forerunner of Jesus, was pure. Because John had a praying mother, he could preach repentance.

Jochebed was Moses' mother and a woman of integrity. She dedicated and protected her son for the great work of leading the children of Israel.

Dorcas was a person of service and served the church by sewing garments for those in need.

The Bible tells us that Lydia opened her house for Paul to stay there while he was preaching in her town.

Then we also have the example of Rebecca, who deceived her husband with her favorite son. Deception was carried over into several generations. Mothers should never have favorites among their children.

Jezebel was an ungodly woman and the downfall of many godly men. She is a stark example of what an evil influence can do by appealing to her husband's ego. She helped in the death of Naboth and took his vineyard for the King.

In Ezekiel 16:44, the Bible tells us, "as is the mother, so is her daughter"! What a challenge.

Motherhood is a constant job—we don't vacation from it. A husband provides for the family and therefore leaves the mother with the greater responsibility of teaching and training the children.

Proverbs 31 reminds us that motherhood is for life . . . "all the days of her life."

A mother needs to be a disciplinarian. That seems to be lacking in our society. Mothers need to call to account misdeeds as they arise, rather than saying, "As soon as Daddy gets home, you'll be punished!" Often this is used as an excuse not to deal with a misdeed right away.

How does the child respond to having this guilt hanging over him all day? As the day advances, the guilt and fear keep him from looking forward to his daddy's return from work. How much better it would be if the mother would deal consistently with the wrong and clear the child from guilt. He would look forward to seeing his daddy rather than fearing his return.

Too often the wrong is forgotten and the punishment never meted out when Daddy comes home. Therefore the child gets the feeling that perhaps he will be able to get by again. That builds a wall instead of a bridge to open communication.

Threatening should not prevail in the Christian home. Consistency is a must! We are laying a solid foundation early in life when we are consistent in saying "Yea, yea," or "Nay, nay," and sticking with it. If your word does not bring the desired results the first time, then get up from that recliner and bring correction. It will not take much, and our children will know that we mean what we say.

It has been a policy in our home, to tell Daddy of a misdeed together, child and mother. Even when a glass was broken, I encouraged the children to tell Daddy. That has brought an open communication down through the years.

Another policy our family has is that, whenever feasible, we all go shopping together. The children learned to respect our wishes in buying clothes and other items. There were times as they grew older and my minister husband's workload got heavier that the children and I would do the shopping for clothes and other items. But if Daddy was not along, we would buy the item with the stipulation that it first needed to meet his approval. In this way we as a family were respecting the head of our home.

One time stands out in my mind when we had the blessing of having a good working together as a family. Our teenaged son was building a gun cabinet, his first piece of furniture, and he asked me to go with him to a fabric store to choose a piece of velvet that would accent the furniture. On the way home we stopped at McDonald's and had lunch together. Another time he felt the need of my help in selecting a piece of velvet for a gift he was making for his girlfriend.

We have been married twenty-five years and our children are nearly grown, but the girls still invite me to go to town with them. They seem to enjoy that.

What a blessing and what a reward for those hard and trying times when it would have seemed easy to throw up my hands! God's grace was sufficient to bring me to the time of my life when I can rejoice in faithful children that are open to communicate and share. It far outweighs any fears or frustrations that were involved in being a mother.

The following are some qualities that constitute a strong family:

A. Be committed to each other—husband/wife, parents/children
B. Spend time together
C. Have good, open communication
D. Often express appreciation for each other
E. Have a deepening spiritual commitment to God
F. Be able to work through problems in a crisis

Deuteronomy 6:1-5 mentions four basic principles that keep the family strong. We need to *teach* God's commandments and statutes and judgments; we must *fear* the Lord; our ears must be in tune with God's Word so we can *hear*; and we must *love* the Lord with all our heart, soul and might. These principles cancel out any room for self. There is a definite connection between forsaking God's truth and broken homes. Self is the object that breaks the home. Someone said, "Let there be a revival of the family and we will regain the spiritual resources so badly needed."

One of the neglected virtues of motherhood is being authentic (genuine, worthy of acceptance, trustworthy). Here are some steps to help you be more authentic: (1) If you are not sure, admit it! (2) If you are afraid of the risk, say so! (3) If you don't know the answer to a question your child asks, say "I don't know," but be open to help them find answers and go back to them. (4) If you are wrong, confess it! (5) If you feel under pressure, own up to it! (6) If your children ask why, and you really don't have an answer, refuse to dodge behind that confidence-shattering cliche, "Because I said so"! If we really don't have a better answer than that, perhaps we need to bend and give in.

Let's take a look at one home setting. The minister and his wife spent considerable time with a person who was at the brink of despair. In the meantime, the minister's children were becoming anxious. There was a program in the area which they wanted to attend, and the time was nearing for it to begin. (They had asked earlier, but received no answer.) Out of respect for their parents, they were not going to attend without their permission.

When the teenagers asked again, they received a curt answer, "No!" without any open and honest sharing. Later, when they asked why, they were told "Because I said so!" The results: unhappy, rejected teenagers; curt and critical parents; communication lines broken, and confidence shattered.

We as parents need to answer our children's questions honestly and lovingly. It may take some time to answer their questions, but they are as important as any other person in need. All too often our children only get our "leftover" time.

There is no need for despair. "If any of you lack

wisdom, let [her] ask of God, that gives to all [women] liberally or generously without finding fault. And wisdom will be given to [her]" (James 1:5, paraphased). God does not accept excuses! If we lack wisdom, ask God!

Twentieth century women can do no greater thing than to create a climate of love in their homes. But—

Love that spoils and pampers
Weakens and hampers.

Real love strengthens and matures and leaves the loved one free to grow!

Homemaker's Prayer

Lord, you have chosen me for the noblest of woman's callings. I ask You for wisdom to use well my opportunity. May the precious lives entrusted to Your care blossom to beauty and maturity in this home. Grant that they may come from the world's rough and thorny ways to find rest and a secure, loving family. May they be renewed each day in faith, hope and love. May we live for the best and highest, seeking to lessen, where we can, the burdens of others. Strengthen me, but keep me soft-hearted and tolerant of others. Make me willing to learn from the old as well as from the young. Dear Lord, make me sufficient for my task.

—Author Unknown

Homemaking, A Full-Time Job

by Anna Mary (Mrs. Bennie) Byler

It is true—a woman can handle many of man's jobs and do them well. When she becomes dissatisfied with one job, she can quit and get another job. But not so with homemaking. It is uniquely a woman's job. It is a full-time job, requiring her all, "all the days of her life." (See Proverbs 31:10-31.)

The women of the greatest power and strength are not those popular in society or those whose names flash on the screens or in the news media. But rather, it is those who allow God to have first place in their hearts and lives. It is those who have dedicated themselves to make a home from the house that has been entrusted to their care.

Women's world today seems dominated by major achievements in academics, in technology, in science. But our communities would be hopeless and helpless without homemakers who spend many hours doing the menial tasks of washing dishes, sweeping floors, washing and mending clothes, rocking babies, doing the grocery shopping and performing dozens of other commonplace tasks. These activities are not homemaker's goals—not ends in themselves, but means to an end of a comfortable home and a happy, responsible family.

Many a mother has performed her tasks well and achieved fame because she was willing to graciously and lovingly do her work behind the scenes.

Abraham Lincoln made this comment: "All that I am and hope to be, I owe to my angel mother." "Surely her children rise up, and call her blessed; her husband also, and he praiseth her" (Provers 31:28).

The key to your contentment and joy is your attitude toward God, yourself, and your role as a homemaker.

The Bible also has much to say concerning the role of the homemaker. She is to be *discreet, chaste,* a *keeper at home, good, obedient* to her own husband, *sober, loving* her husband and children, so God's Word will not be blasphemed (blamed, or spoken of irreverently).

Discreet means having or showing good discernment and good judgment in conduct and speech; unpretentious, modest. I am challenged that Webster refers to discretion as the *warmth* and *elegance* of a *civilized home!*

Chaste would indicate pure in thought and act; free from all taint of what is lewd; having control of one's impulses and actions.

A *keeper at home* is one who keeps, a custodian, one fit or suitable to be a keeper, a protector, good, of a favorable character and tendency, profitable, advantageous, agreeable, pleasant, wholesome, well-founded.

Obedient is being submissive to the restraint or command of authority, and here it would be to submit willingly and cheerfully to our husbands.

Sober is marked by an earnest thoughtful character, unhurried, calm, marked by temperance, moderation and seriousness.

Love is an affection based on admiration, benevolence,

and common interest, unselfish loyalty, benevolent concern for the good of another.

If we are homemakers are to enjoy our role, we must take a positive approach. We must see a half glass of milk as half full, not half empty; see the doughnut, not the hole. Life is much happier when we look for and see the positive side and enjoy the view along the way.

All of the requirements in the Bible for being a faithful homemaker are positive. God has our good in mind as He instructs us in the best way He planned for the Christian family.

Homemaking is much more than a job. It is a noble and honorable profession and of the highest benefit to mankind. We dare not forget this, although we are not on a payroll. Nevertheless, we must be conscious of our calling before God, and the tremendous contribution that we can make to His Kingdom in our chosen role as homemaker.

Family life weakens when Mother becomes bored or self-centered. The mother plays a vital role in the general atmosphere of the home!

Why does a homemaker become bored when God has blessed her with a house she can call her castle, her own family (a gift from the Lord), health and strength to work and care for her most precious family?

Why does a homemaker dread the daily, humble tasks, that require no college education or degrees? Yet at her disposal is God's grace and strength to carry out those daily tasks.

Why does a homemaker dread the constant chore of washing dishes, cleaning floors and windows? God tells us in His Word, "Whatsoever thy hand findeth to do, do it with thy might; . . ." (Eccl. 9:10a).

Why is it so easy to put off doing today what we

should do, thinking, "tomorrow I'll have more time"? Why not do all we can today, because we "know not what shall be on the morrow" (James 4:14a)?

It is much easier to pick up the toys, straighten up the house, and wash the dishes before we retire, than to face those neglected tasks, plus doing our regular work, in the morning.

In a wedding message many years ago, a minister mentioned the importance of cleaning up the house every evening before going to bed. He said that while his mother washed the dishes and straightened up the house, she would say, "Boys, pick up your toys, because we never know if one of us may die before morning." If this procedure is followed, any homemaker is "miles ahead" the next morning.

Who feels like getting up to a kitchen of chaos and trying to prepare a nourishing breakfast? No one feels like it and, generally speaking, no one does it. The homemaker is defeated before she ever gets out of bed, not to mention how this affects her husband and children. No wonder there are frustrated and irresponsible children going to school and teenagers going to work in a disheartened mood, if the homemaker has not died to self, allowing God to reign. We need to live for God and our family.

Why is it so easy to half-heartedly go through the day and neglect daily devotions in the morning? And yet we wonder why we are so disorganized, frustrated, so easily peeved or discouraged. Psalm 5:3 reminds us "My voice shalt thou hear in the morning, O Lord; in the morning will I direct my prayer unto thee and will look up." Someone made the challenging remark, "We cannot remain discouraged, when we look up!"

Why not begin now and ask God to help you see Him

in everything as you wash those diapers, bathe the baby, wash the dishes, sweep the floor, pick up and do the laundry? "And whatsoever ye do in word or deed, do all in the name of the Lord Jesus, giving thanks to God and the Father by him" (Col. 3:17).

If we see homemaking "as unto the Lord" it will change our bored, selfish, careless, dreading attitude into a cheerful, thankful, caring and giving outlook in life. Then it will be easy to carry out those same, lowly duties of everyday homemaking.

A Prayer For Womankind

God, give each true good woman
    Her own small house to keep—
No heart should ache with longing,
    No hurt should go too deep—
Grant her age-old desire:
    A house to love and sweep.

Give her a man beside her—
    A kind man—and a true–
And let them work together
    And love—a lifetime through,
And let her mother children
    As gentle women do.

God, let her work with laughter,
    And let her rest with sleep—
No life can truly offer
    A peace more sure and deep—
God, give each true woman
    Her own small house to keep.

—Grace Noll Cromwell

The Ministry Of Christian Womanhood

by Barbara (Mrs. Dan) Yoder

Welcome to the ministers' meeting! Each one of us is a minister. All of us have a work to do, an area of service in which God has called us to work—that is our ministry. We all know the feeling of being swamped with duties and responsibilities. Our lives are made up of a lot of everyday tasks that need to be done over and over again. We tend to forget that we are making small daily investments in the lives of our families and those around us that add up to either enriching their lives or hindering the development of their character.

For our ministry to be truly unlimited, there are three people that we will need to accept. The first one is Jesus Christ. We have heard the plan of salvation over and over again; we know what it takes; we've been taught all our lives. But the fact still remains that having Jesus Christ as Saviour and Lord of our lives is the first and most basic requirement for usefulness in this life. With Him in control, all the power of God is at our aid! We need to yield our lives completely and allow His Holy Spirit to control our very being. With the fruit of the Spirit in our lives there will be no limit. No one will ever say, "That's enough love or joy now —no more," or "She has far too much temperance." The Spirit ministers through us to those around us and His power is unlimited. That is what makes our ministry unlimited.

We need to unreservedly ask God to work out His will in our lives every day. We dare not keep back any area for ourselves. The very area we reserve, not allowing Him to use, will eventually become our downfall. Moses told the Lord that he couldn't talk. God said, "I will be with your mouth." But Moses persisted, and God agreed to send Aaron to speak for him. Later, at the rock, it was Moses' tongue that got him into trouble when he struck the rock angrily. If he would have given his tongue to the Lord from the beginning, he would have been allowed to enter the promised land. Can we give Him our plans, our purposes and our preferences? Can we ask Him to use us, to fill us, to work out His will in our lives only as He wills? Or is there a limit or a certain area that we reserve as our own property that is not accessible to God?

It is rather scary to give everything. We have the idea that God is just waiting to take us and shake us up, and make us do something that we don't want to do. But do we find peace in insisting on our own way? Of course not! Peace only comes through yielding. Psalm 145:17 says, "The Lord is righteous in all his ways, and holy in all his works." We can trust Him to work out all that is best for us, even though it shakes us up at times, and the task is unpleasant to our flesh. Our prayer needs to be that He may be glorified in everything.

The second person we need to accept is ourselves; first as the person that God made. Are you thankful for how God made you—your looks, personality, circumstances? God has created each one of us in His own image for a special purpose. We tend to equate God's love to us with the love of those around us; however, we dare not compare

God's love with human love. We may not feel how special we are to Him, because we do not feel very special to those around us, but our feelings are not an accurate measurement of the facts.

When we feel this way, we look around for someone to blame. "My parents are the cause of this complex that I have, if only they would have been different," "I'm sanguine, that is why I'm so unorganized," or, "I'm melancholy, that explains my moodiness."

When we make excuses and blame others, we are only saying that our problem is too big for God to handle; He just can't solve my problem. Will He make a special exception for anyone? This is unbelief. God has put each one of us in the very place He wants us to be, to work out His special purpose. Remember, life is not always fair; God does not give each one of us identical circumstances; like we give our children an equal amount of candy. But He gives His grace more than fairly, He gives it abundantly —there's no limit! God wants to use the trying times we face as a means of showing His glory. Let's count our blessings and recognize that God is working.

We also need to accept ourselves as women. Are we sorry that we are women? Do we wish for equal rights so that some things would be done right for a change? The world tells us we need rights; there is no difference in the sexes; it is all a matter of conditioning.

But the fact remains that God intended for woman to be submissive.

As we live in submission we will find true freedom. Trying to lead and be like men will only bring us into bondage. God's plan from the beginning was to make woman for the man—to complete him. Psalm 144:12 says, "That our daughters may be as pillars, sculptured in palace style" (NKJ). Pillars uphold and support. They make the building beautiful. This is our ministry as women. Just as a pillar is shaped and cut to fit into a particular place, and carry a specified weight, just that precisely we have been created to fill a special role.

Mary was a supreme example of human self-giving. She said, "Behold the handmaid of the Lord; be it unto me according unto thy word" (Luke 1:38). All her life, and since, she was well known only because she was Jesus' mother. Our response needs to be the same as hers.

How is the Christian woman's ministry different because she is a woman and not a man? It is mainly through her submission, which ministers to the needs of man. But it is also through the tenderness and sympathy, which are more natural for women than for men. A woman in her God-given place, softens and beautifies the rough and coarse parts of this world. This then, is our ministry as women: kindness, sympathy, tenderness, support, and yes, submission. As we follow God's plan we will be able to be an unlimited blessing to those around us.

Thirdly, we need to accept others. Without others, there would, of course, be no ministry! Just as God created us as people of His design, even so He has made everyone else. Not accepting others is a personal bitterness and rebellion against God: "Why did you make them so?" It is hard to understand some people, but not accepting and loving them is to show a self-righteous attitude: "I am better than they." It is in direct disobedience to the command, "Love one another." How do we love those who are hard to love? Through them we learn what real love is all about. We need to realize that at times we ourselves may be hard to love. Let's treat others as we would like to be treated.

God does not wait to use us until we are perfect. And He uses other imperfect people to work out His will in our own lives. Rahab was a harlot, and she lied. But God used her to help Israel conquer Jericho, and after her conversion He also used her in the lineage of Jesus.

We need to pray and ask God to give us love. This is a lot like praying for patience. What is the first thing that comes to our mind when patience is what we really need? Aren't we inclined to pray for a change of circumstances instead? But do we receive patience or love without praying for it and asking God to work out His will in our lives?

It is a much greater blessing to pray that God may work His love in our lives, and not cringe in fear of the tests that will come. But we can look back at the end of the day and see how God worked in us without our awareness. Then let's thank Him and continue to give ourselves to Him. If we are truly open to God, His Spirit will lead us, in revealing our own need, and also our relationships with others. As we follow Him, He will lead us on step by step. The Christian life is a love relationship with Jesus Christ and not a mere list of regulations. He will lead us into all truth (John 16:13).

Elizabeth Elliot said it well: "We are called to be women. The fact that I am a woman does not make me a different kind of Christian. But the fact that I am a Christian makes me a different kind of woman. For I have accepted God's idea of me, and my whole life is an offering back to Him of all that I am and all he wants me to be."

About The Writer

Barbara is the oldest child in her family. Her mother died of cancer when Barbara was 14 years old, leaving her responsible for her siblings.

Five months after her mother's death, her father was ordained deacon of the Maple Lawn Church in Nappenee, Indiana. Barbara then took her responsibility seriously to encourage her dad in his ministry.

In 1971 Barbara met Dan Yoder. They both served several years at Faith Mission Home—a home for the mentally handicapped children.

After their marriage in December, 1972, Dan served as assistant administrator, and later as administrator, of Faith Mission Home.

In May of 1987, he was ordained deacon at Pilgrim Fellowship in Stuarts Draft, Virginia. Earlier in 1986, they had moved there to help his dad on a turkey farm.

They have five children, which makes Barbara a busy homemaker. She also assists her husband in his responsibilities. As a hobby, she enjoys piecing quilts.

The Preacher's Wife

There is one person in your church
    Who knows your preacher's life;
She's wept and smiled and prayed with him,
    And that's your preacher's wife!

She knows your prophet's weakest points,
    And knows his greatest power;
She's heard him speak in trumpet tone
    In his great triumph hour.

She's heard him groaning in his soul
    When bitter raged the strife.
As, hand in his she knelt with him—
    For she's the preacher's wife!

The crowd has seen him in his strength,
    When glistened his drawn sword;
As underneath God's banner folds
    He faced the devil's horde.

But she knows deep within her heart
    That scarce an hour before
She helped him pray the glory down
    Behind a fast-closed door.

You tell your tales of prophets brave
    Who walked across the world,
And changed the course of history
    By burning words they hurled.

And I will tell how back of them
    Some women lived their lives;
Who wept with them, and prayed with them—
    They were the preachers' wives.

—*Author Unknown*

Accepting The Role Of Minister's Wife

by Anna Mary (Mrs. Bennie) Byler

C an you accept your husband's calling as of the Lord? Will you promise to support your husband? These are two questions that are asked at an ordination, and there is no one who has any idea what all this may include. How thankful we as ministers' wives can be that God does not "dump" the reponsibility into our laps and leave us with no guidelines to follow.

In this chapter we will endeavor to share some guidelines that may be of assistance to those whom God has just recently called to this great work as a minister's wife. Then there are those of you who have experienced years of being co-workers with your husbands, so perhaps to you this chapter can be an encouragement to not grow weary in the work of the Lord. Or there is a possibility that some need a rekindling of dedication to this awesome responsibility.

This call as a minister's wife is not for a year like some other offices. It's not just temporary, but to the faithful it is a lifetime commitment and it is up to us as individuals what we are going to do with it.

Our response in practice to the questions of whether we can accept our husband's calling and support him in it, can either make or break him.

Perhaps the most important qualification for a faithful minister's wife is total dedication. This means commitment, giving God the controls or "rolling" our will and work over onto the Lord.

Psalm 37 reminds us to commit our way to the Lord and then also to rest in the Lord.

Joshua 1:8 tells of the importance of not letting the Bible or "book of the law" depart out of our mouth. If we do according to all that is written therein, "then we shall make our way prosperous, and we shall gave good success." The following verse is then ours to claim. "Be strong and of a good courage; be not afraid, neither be thou dismayed: for the Lord thy God is with thee whithersover thou goest" (Joshua 1:9).

Why should we even have a thought of fear or anxiety? The One who made us and knows us far better than we know ourselves, has also called us to this high and holy calling and it is only reasonable service to present our bodies a living sacrifice (Rom. 12:1).

As the faithful wife of a minister we must again and again remind ourselves that we "are not our own" neither is our husband ours, but we are bought with a price (I Cor. 6:19-20). With this perspective in view, the work of the minister will be high on our list of priorities.

A minister's wife may experience unique testings, but we need not despair; for by our fellowship with God and by keeping busy, we can by God's grace rise above these petty irritations that would bring defeat to our lives.

Like her minister husband, the wife must feel the call to his ministry if she wishes to give herself to a life of service for God and the people. Together they should look at the ministry as the noblest work in the world. What greater blessing is there to share, than in the saving of a sin-sick soul or rejoicing with one who has just experienced a victory in his life?

If we want God's blessings on the ministry of our husbands, then our call is that of being first of all a faithful wife and mother. A mother should cherish motherhood above any other position on earth.

A radiant Christian personality is important, as we cast our cares on the Lord. We do not need to look as if we were carrying the burden alone.

A neat person is one who is concerned about her appearance, and therefore soap and water are important. Body odor is offensive to say the least, and if deodorant irritates the skin then a sufficient amount of soap and water will prevent any odor. Our clothes need not be the best, but they should be clean and in harmony with our Christian life, remembering that the minister's wife should represent the Lord and His church in the community.

"The story is told of a saintly minister, who was laboring over the details of his attire, when at last he explained, 'God has not given me a handsome body, but my body is the temple of the Holy Spirit, and I want it and my linen to be neat and clean, for so holy a guest. Especially when I go to the pulpit do I wish to be worthy of the King.' " (*The Pastor's Wife,* by Carolyn Blackwood).

This should be a challenge for us, that if God's Spirit lives within, then it also is evident by our modest, neat, clean dress. We also should help and encourage our husband in this area.

Someone has said, "I can tell a lot about you, by the way you walk." So we need to be of gracious composure. Our voice should be pleasant. We should speak clearly and distinctly. Our voice should not change depending to whom we are talking. Our children and husband need to hear the same pleasant voice that our neighbors do. One who is loud and boastful, is not a woman of a meek and quiet spirit.

We need to guard against a coarse or impatient tone of voice. At times we do have frustrations. Perhaps the phone rings repeatedly and we are tempted to become irritable or curt. We must remember the person calling has no idea that theirs is the tenth call we answered in the last hour. A minister's wife must have a love for all people, a compassionate heart, and always be courteous.

Common sense is a much needed ingredient in the life of a minister's wife. She must be cool-headed and level-minded. This is next to piety and loving kindness. We are often called on to share, and if we will be an encouragement we must have a vital relationship with our Lord.

Love, sympathy, common sense, and courtesy are all virtues that make the minister's wife the influential person God desires her to be. If we by faith cultivate these virtues the Lord will still add others. As we grow in grace, we will be able to accept criticism with poise and gratitude.

We must continually be aware of the importance of keeping our homes orderly and comfortable in order to welcome our husband home. One minister remarked to his wife, "How could I ever keep going with my work if you did not have the home inviting and comfortable when I come home after a hard day?"

Words of appreciation can be an eye opener and we need to be reminded that the work of a minister does not consist in freedom from care. If any woman "will come after me, let [her] deny [her]self, and take up [her] cross, and follow me" (Mark 8:34).

Possibly many of us were called to the role of motherhood before becoming a minister's wife, so our first duty is to make our home a pleasant and attractive place for our families. The same holds true for any woman, but especially the minister's wife, "the observed of all observers."

There are several rules, that, if applied, will save embarrassment and can add relaxation to the family and visitors alike.

a. Practice keeping the living room neat and clean, making it the norm.

b. If you have a guest room, make it a habit to clean and change sheets soon after the former guests leave, so you need not go into a frenzy to straighten up the room and change sheets, when unexpected guests arrive.

c. It's a good policy to have the bathroom clean for your family, but how repulsive to see a dirty, stained toilet or a tub with particles or rings of a bygone bath. (When a child is old enough to take his own bath, he is also old enough to clean the tub.)

d. Keep the bathroom cabinets orderly and have towels for guests to use. Even small children can learn how to fold the towels properly. If we teach the children they will perform as they are taught.

The following story is taken from *The Pastor's Wife*, by Carolyn Blackwood, pages 46-47.

"A minister and his wife were visiting at a neighboring church and were guests at the minister's house. The visitors found the porch littered with tricycles, garden tools, and mud splattered on the floor. The study was in shambles, with books in disarray; the living room topsy-turvy with newspapers, toys, and sewing scattered about; the bathroom full of filth; open doors showed beds unmade, soiled clothes and dirty furnishings; finger marks on the walls and elsewhere.

"The wife explained that she was so busy helping at

the church that she had to neglect the house, but surely all that disorder and dirt did not accumulate over night! Anyhow, if a woman feels she ought to leave her house in disorder and dirt while she does 'the work of the Lord,' she has a dislocated sense of duty! If any woman cannot render such service without neglecting her home and family, then let the claims of the home come first. Before she looks elsewhere for openings to do good, let her set her own house in order. After guests have come and gone, whether she had known of their coming or not, may she hear the voice of the Lord whisper, 'What have they seen in thy house?' ." We may be guilty of discrediting our husbands and be a discouragement to them, making it hard to preach practical, everyday messages if we are not clean and neat house keepers.

We should be examples of gracious living, yet at times we all need to be reminded of the above story to help us set our priorities straight.

Long-range planning is the secret of "effortless ease." So is habit! Planning makes for order and relaxation.

Two things to remember, when we have guests is to make everyone feel at ease and happy in your home, and don't criticize your guests to family members after they have left.

I suppose many a hostess has found notes after the guests have gone. How encouraging! We should never seek glory for ourselves, but in the area of being a hostess, our goal should be "as unto the Lord," never to draw attention to oneself.

Years ago when our children were small, there were times I would get frustrated about finding time for my private devotions. Finally after lots of struggling, I made it a point to spend a short time in meditation just as soon as the children left for school. The baby would be awake, but I would take her along and place her on the bed while I would kneel and pray. I prayed orally at times and often she fell asleep and took her morning nap.

Years ago, someone made the comment, "more is done to affect the moral and religious character of children before the age of language, than after!" How very true this statment is, so fill the sub-conscious with ideas and stories about God and Jesus.

We should be like Susanna Wesley: know the value of repetition, precept upon precept, line upon line, over and over again. We dare not leave to chance the most important part of life!

It's no easy task to raise a family and the minister's family is no exception; but we can be assured where God leads, there His grace will be sufficient.

There are many blessings in store for the young mother who is cheerful and willing to stay at home when the children are sick, while her minister husband goes to preach with peace in his heart and the assurance that he is undergirded with prayer.

One of the greatest blessings is the personal time alone with the sick child. Not only will it draw mother and child together, but it will be a time of undivided attention to the child that will always be cherished. Then also what better time for the special touch, a cold drink to a feverish mouth, or the back rub to a sore and restless child. A quiet Sunday morning or evening can be refreshing to the mother, to know that she can still draw from the "fountain of life" while caring for the sick. Memories are made during times like these that last a life time.

Every Christian family should find time for family devotions. When the children are small we should seek to make it short, but interesting. Teach the little ones to sit still. To small children it should be their "little church."

The spirit of devotions can be shattered by the attitude of a busy mother. "Once you're ready for devotions I'll come!" The attitude is apparent: "Work is the main thing, but when you say so we'll stop long enough to fling a moment to God!" How sad! True worship is not an act, but an attitude.

There will be times when the phone will take the husband away from breakfast and devotions, and then it is important that Mother takes over and shares in worship. If the mother does not do this there will be frustrations and insecurities that have an effect on our children. It may even instill on their minds that family devotions fit in only when suitable, and that other things are more important.

In church service we as ministers' wives must seek to develop the gift of encouragement, the tact of acknowledging everyone with a hearty hand shake, and addressing each one by name. The little children also love to be noticed and hear their name, and a pat on their shoulder is reaffirming.

We are not called upon to do all the work, but to encourage, teaching other women by example to employ their gifts in the service of Christ. If we are faithful in encouraging, the work will go on even though we ourselves are not always present.

Many of us are busy. Therefore chairing the monthly sewing circle should be delegated to other sisters in the church. Our presence does say a lot, if we are an encouragement when present. Perhaps there are times when the minister's wife knows of a need, and by sharing with the chairperson the work can be accomplished without the one who suggested it being in the "lime light" or focus.

Another matter that affects the minister and his family more than most other families is the area of criticism. A quote read recently is "Life is a grindstone. Whether it grinds you down or polishes you up depends on what you are made of." This is true about criticism. Constructive criticism should never be taken as a threat, but welcomed as a challenge to search out the facts about yourself or your family. Be open, share, and spend time in prayer. Often through sharing and being open, misunderstandings can be understood, and mistakes corrected.

When we are admonished and found to be at fault, we need to be woman enough to say, "I'm sorry, please forgive me." Confession, if needed, is good for the soul and makes us more careful in how we live.

Some years ago a minister family was criticized for their orderly and neat home. After spending time in prayer the minister couple met with the offended one. The wife expressed her desires for this person to also experience the blessing and benefits that are theirs, and "the wrinkles were ironed out."

Jealousy can often be the hidden obstacle that eats away at the soul. We need to approach such matters in meekness and humility.

One precaution I want to share is that we ministers' wives need to be open and easily entreated, as James tells us. Once another sister offers accusations about the whole family, it would be better if each husband would be included in the discussion. At times, if this approach is taken the accusing sister will not be so critical, or take so much into her own hands.

Malicious words hurt and leave deep wounds. We, as ministers' wives, must ask God to "keep the door of our lips." We need wisdom from God to say the right words, at the right time, in the right spirit.

We all need to deal with malicious remarks at time, and they hurt. In order to help, we need to find out what lies behind the criticism. We must deal lovingly with it, as we would have God deal with us. In any case, accept the challenge. Before you decide what to do "take it to the Lord in prayer." He will guide and sustain you if you let Him. "In quietness and confidence shall be your strength" (Isa. 30:15).

At times the work of the ministry is overwhelming, but we can have this confidence, "Thus saith the Lord; Refrain thy voice from weeping, and thine eyes from tears: for thy work shall be rewarded, saith the Lord" (Jer. 31:16).

The person
who bows the lowest
in the
presence of God
stands the straightest
in the
presence of sin.

FIRST: He brought me here; it is by
          His will I am in this strait
          place; in that will I rest.

NEXT: He will keep me here in His
          love, and give my grace in
          this trial to behave as His child.

THEN: He will make the trial a
          blessing, teaching me the lessons
          He intends me to learn,
          and working in me the grace
          He means to bestow.

LAST: In His good time, He can
          bring me out again—how
          and when, He knows.

SAY: I AM HERE—
          By God's appointment,
          In His keeping,
          Under His training,
          For His time.

Call upon me in the day of trouble:
I will deliver thee,
and thou shalt glorify me (Psalm 50:15).
                              —Andrew Murray

Unrealistic Expectations

by Ernest & Mary Ellen Hochstetler

The bishop's voice was clear to all in the audience as he prayed for my husband who had just been ordained to the office of deacon. The prayer continued on to involve me as the wife. His voice showed a slight hesitation as he prayed for my faithfulness in being a proper and godly deacon's wife. He prayed that I would be a supportive and reliable companion. As I was wondering what all I would be facing, I heard a more pronounced hesitation as he attempted to include our three children in the prayer. Then there was a moment of silence as a sob escaped.

Tears filled our eyes as well as many others in the congregation as we realized that our family's life as well as our church life would be affected. Questions churned through my mind. Could I be that support referred to in the prayer of the officiating bishop? Could and would the children respond to this calling in a loving and understanding way? Were these expectations of our family realistic?

During the time they were small children in the home, their childhood sicknesses and accidents seemed in almost direct conflict with my husband's calling. Why should these burdens be added to the support that was already expected of me? The answer became clear as I recalled the many "unplanned and unexplainables" in the Bible where mothers were asked to give of themselves in the Lord's service in more than one area of their lives. Those times also gave me contact with other mothers who were struggling with a busy life. My husband's ordination did not make him or me superhuman.

Being involved in a voluntary service unit for several years called for demands and schedules that were overwhelmingly great, and at times in conflict with each other. The quality of our time together as a family became of utmost importance. Many times we noticed other families having a greater quantity of time together, which brought feelings of dissatisfaction. Comparing ourselves among ourselves, even in this matter, is not wise.

As years passed, the children grew into young adulthood, and their understanding of our calling increased as well. Their concepts and views gained through observing the struggles and victories of our ministry have become a valuable part of their decision making. They gained in spiritual maturity through this and also the influence of their peers and others who set examples.

In the early years parents influence their children. We tell them what to do and what not to do. When they are grown, who influences whom? That question rang through my mind as my husband was preparing for another preaching assignment away from home. As I anticipated traveling with him, I was emotionally quite involved in the needs of our family and pressures around home.

Our car needed to be taken to the shop for repairs. My emotions were running high as our daughter and I neared the edge of town. When tears followed this emotional stress, I became aware of the change taking place in our family in the recent years. The tables were turning. There at that car shop our daughter was ministering to my needs.

As she encouraged me to look beyond the present conflicts and busy schedule, her encouragement was gratefully received by my spirit and was soothing and healing.

This experience seemed to confirm God's promise that He will help us carry our cross, and that His yoke is easy and His burden is light. God provided through our daughter the emotional help I was in need of. Similar incidents have repeatedly taken place in recent years and serve as a real stimulus to fight the good fight of faith that Paul encouraged Timothy to fight (1 Timothy 6:12).

For the minister's family to rise to the full expectations of "Dad's calling," a strong commitment to interfamily communication must be established as a priority. This will not happen automatically. The family must work together on it.

Areas I Would Like to Explore

1. It is often considered to be primarily the duty of the ordained minister and his family to entertain those within and without the church. While the calling to be "hospitable" is for all members of the church, there is the need for us to be an example. The atmosphere for either "unforced" willingness or resentment at having to get a meal together or changing sheets for unexpected company is often set by a mother/wife's own attitude. Thus the example of being hospitable is dependent on our maintaining a cheerful and willing attitude.

2. What about frequent requests for special meetings where the ordained husband is taken away from the family for several days, a week or even longer? Should the husband sometimes say "No" or always say "Yes."? Someone must respond to the calls.

   We live in an age where the word vacation has

become a part of our vocabulary and many families enjoy the experience of camping together. Occasionally we as a family will make an assignment of my husband's a family trip as well, where we all go along and the experience becomes a multi-benefit. It helps to support Dad in his preaching and gives the children the opportunity to see that not every community and situation is just like our own. Especially is this true if the call comes to go to some other country. Such trips have enriched our lives and helped to replace the times of family camping, etc.

3. Needs within the congregation frequently demand special meetings and counseling sessions. Our families can have a very negative feeling toward such needs if we totally refrain from any sharing. This is, however, no suggestion that we openly discuss the issues and problems with our children, but rather that we use discretion as we share, so they can better support us in our involvement with prayer. They will be more understanding and will put forth more effort to make it easier for Dad and Mom to have time for those needs. And what a blessing when they encourage us to keep on! As our family prays together on various matters we often find meaningful thoughts, views and insights for those immediate needs.

Are these expectations unrealistic? Not when we see how our attitudes and responses affect Dad's ministry! Our strengths can become his strengths. May we rise to the challenge of that calling.

About the Writers

Prior to their marriage Ernest and Mary Ellen were both involved in various voluntary service programs. Ernest spent two years in Central America as one of the first missionaries to El Salvador, under Amish Mennonite Aid. They were married on March 30, 1968. On April 23, 1972, Ernest was ordained deacon.

They have taken their church responsibilities very seriously and have been a means of challenging and encouraging many people.

Ernest has been teaching the past six years in their church school, and Mary Ellen is a homemaker and a companion in Ernest's duties and responsibilities.

With their family of four children they reside in Abbeville, South Carolina.

What Is Maturity?

Maturity is the ability to control anger and settle differences without violence or destruction.

Maturity is patient. It is the willingness to pass up immediate pleasure in favor of the long-term gain.

Maturity is perseverance, the ability to sweat out a project or a situation in spite of hearing oppositions and discouraging set backs.

Maturity is the capacity to face unpleasantness and frustration, discomfort and defeat, without complaint or collapse.

Maturity is humility. It is being big enough to say "I was wrong." And when right, the mature person will not want to experience the satisfaction of saying "I told you so!"

Maturity is the ability to make a decision and stand by it. The immature spend their lives exploring endless possibilities; then they do nothing.

Maturity means dependability, keeping one's word, coming through a crisis. The immature are masters of the alibi. They are the confused and disorganized. Their lives are "mazes of broken promises, former friends, unfinished business and good intentions that somehow never materialize."

Maturity is the art of living in peace with that which we cannot change, the courage to change that which *should* be changed—and the wisdom to know the difference.

original source unknown—has appeared in Ann Landers

Living In A Glass House

by Anna Mary (Mrs. Bennie) Byler

"Blessed is every one that feareth the Lord; that walketh in His ways. For thou shalt eat the labor of thine hands: happy shalt thou be, and it shall be well with thee. Thy wife shall be as a fruitful vine by the sides of thy house: thy children like olive plants round about they table. Behold, that thus shall the man be blessed that feareth the Lord. The Lord shall bless thee out of Zion: and thou shalt see the good of Jerusalem all the days of thy life. Yea, thou shalt see thy children's children, and peace upon Israel" (Psalm 128).

Have you ever driven along a road during the daytime, looked at the houses from the outside, and wondered what it is like inside those houses? Are the occupants happy and spending time in prayer and the Word, or are they sad and angry?

Have you ever looked at a town at night, with all the houses well lighted, and wondered how many of the people who live there beam spiritual light by the lives they live?

Our homes, in a sense, are glass houses! Are they also lighthouses—living examples? We are witnessing to those who come to our homes, as well as to those we meet elsewhere. What are we telling the world? What are they seeing?

77

As we allow God to be the center of our homes, and to control our lives, we will always be shining examples of His grace, regardless of circumstances!

Do our homes radiate the kind of atmosphere where troubled souls feel free to come to for help? "We would see Jesus" (Jn. 12:21) expresses a crying need today.

Homes are "set on fire" by an unbridled tongue. "A soft answer turns away wrath, but a harsh word stirs up anger. The tongue of the wise dispenses knowledge, but the mouths of fools pour out folly" (Proverbs 15: 1-2, RSV).

The causes of many broken homes today may be traced to such conflicts as uncontrolled tempers, impatience, hatred, jealousy, or sharp tongues.

The Bible teaches that the person wise enough to hold his or her tongue is a victor. Doing so saves the family from many a crisis. Patience and kindness always pay dividends!

Meeting adversity with courage is only obtained as we humble ourselves, cast all our care on Him, and leave it there. We must be sober and be on guard, then God can make us perfect, stablish, strengthen, and settle us, after we have suffered awhile (I Peter 5:6-10).

The story is told of Ben Franklin, who wanted to install street lighting in the city of Philadelphia. However, he knew the city fathers would refuse to pay the price. So he hung a beautiful lantern on a long bracket in front of his house. Passersby, stumbling in the dark, rejoiced in Franklin's well-lighted area. Soon his neighbors did as he had done. Before long the entire city saw the value of street lighting.

Franklin achieved what he wanted by example, without arguments. One example is worth a thousand arguments. No wonder the Bible says we should "set an example for the believers in speech, in life, in love, in faith and in purity" (I Tim. 4:12, NIV).

Never can we overemphasize the importance of exemplifying Christ in our homes, and living open before God, having nothing to hide. We know that our hearts are as transparent as glass to God, and there is nothing we can hide from Him. We may be able to fool people for a short time, but even they often see more than we are aware of.

Paul said, "Ye are our epistle written in our hearts, known and read of all men" (II Cor. 3:2). To paraphrase it for our day, we could say, "Our homes are known and read of all men."

"Let your light [home] so shine before men, that they may see your good works, and glorify your Father which is in heaven" (Matt. 5:16). It is an awesome responsibility for the home and the family to glorify our heavenly Father.

Perhaps the first step is confidence in God—seeing Him in everything, and recognizing our total dependence on Him. At the same time, we need to live in such a way that, by His grace, we may finish our course with joy.

Security, the second step, is not money in the bank; it is not relying on self, nor having everything money can buy. True security is a personal relationship with God, who will supply all our needs, both physical and spiritual. If we are kept in God's hand, that is security enough. No flood can wash that security away; no tornado can uproot it; nor can any earthquake shake it. That security in God is ours as we meet His conditions. It is there for all of us to reach out and to claim. But the condition we must meet is to turn from the world and to find ourselves in the hollow of God's hand.

The story is told of a little girl who was heard to pray, "Dear Lord, make Mommy as kind to us as she is to the people in town." The mother was amused, and in a joking way related the incident to her husband. He kindly told her that it wasn't a joke, but encouraged her to take a good look at herself.

Perhaps at times we too need to be reminded that those who are nearest to us need to be loved and respected, even more than those with whom we work, or those outside our families.

A good motto for the home: "Christ is the Head of this home, the unseen Host at every meal, the silent Listener to every conversation."

The challenge is also ours to be strong and courageous, not to be afraid or dismayed about the devil and the multitudes with him. There are more with us than with him. With him is the arm of flesh, but with us is the Lord our God to help and fight our battle (II Chron. 32:7, 8).

We may as well admit that the life of a minister's family is in the public eye. This brings both problems and privileges. We must learn that there are no privileges without problems, but we can choose to be motivated by both.

I Peter 5:2 mentions that the leaders must take the oversight of the church, not by constraint, but willingly; not for money, but of a ready mind; neither as lords over God's heritage, but being ensamples to the flock [people].

As we daily love as examples (willing to be a public pattern to copy), and allow adversities to enrich our lives, God can further use us. Our lives become examples or models to follow, because God gives grace to use our circumstances to make us stronger, and to use obstacles as stepping-stones rather than stumbling blocks.

Not everything needs to be in top-notch shape all the time, but a life of order can be a big blessing in a "glass house." Basically, when we as mothers love our children, we will believe deep in our hearts that being a homemaker is our calling. Then those never-ending chores and endless deeds of love make that home a place of refuge from the outside world.

Our husbands and children will enjoy being there. Since Mother loves her "castle," she will be there to welcome the family home after a hard day of labor, office work, school teaching, or going to school; and the whole family will find it a solace. Then not only is the family at ease, but unexpected visitors will also find life in the "glass house" one of comfort and encouragement.

A Christan home is God-centered, family-oriented, a shelter from the evil forces, and a godly refuge where God has placed His hedge of protection around the family. In Job 1:10, Satan recognized such a protection: "Hast thou not made an hedge about him, and about his house, and about all that he hath on every side? Thou has blessed the work of his hands, and his substance is increased in the land."

If Satan recognizes God's hedge, how much more should we as minister families! Then we can say with a note of victory, "Where Christ dwells and the Holy Blood of the Lamb is applied, Satan is put to flight!"

I must admit that living in the spotlight is not easy. We do many things to protect ourselves and our families from public scrutiny. Perhaps we build walls around our houses to keep the arrows of criticism from shattering the glass. God has placed us in the ministry and we dare not withdraw. Yet we are human, and sometimes we become fearful to live as God directs. We dare not allow such feeling to govern our lives!

Any person in responsibility will make mistakes. How thankful we can be that, if we at times fail, God does not cast us down. He's there to help us up and allow our failures to become stepping-stones to a closer walk with Him.

During the past fourteen years my husband has been laboring in the ministry, and the qualifications for a minister are often read and expounded. I often read I Timothy 3, seeking to conform my life to the standard God expects of the minister's wife. The passage points clearly to some awesome responsibilities. The word "blameless" (vv. 2 and 10) always seems to stand out in bold letters. How is the minister's family supposed to be blameless (without fault) when we are so human? I struggled and searched and often felt at a loss, because I knew I could not be without fault. Then at an ordination, several years ago, I was so blessed to hear a minister say that in this passage, "blameless" means "confessed up-to-date!" Then I knew that by God's grace I could achieve that. It has been a real blessing ever since. I do fail, and yet I can confess and ask for forgiveness; then by God's provision I am again blameless.

"Providing for honest things, not only in the sight of the Lord but also in the sight of men" (II Cor. 8:21), is another aspect of living in a glass house. We cannot hide from God, but if we aren't honest with people, how can we be providing things honest before God? We need to be honest and open, realizing that "our sufficiency is of God" (II Cor. 3:5).

Sometimes the minister and his wife need to reassure and encourage their children to maintain good attitudes. How do they feel about living in a glass house? Is it a burden to them, or do they see the challenge as an added blessing? Do our children enjoy unexpected visitors who perhaps make demands? Do they appreciate a rigid schedule and order in our homes? Is it a pressure or a privilege to be identified as minister's children?

All these and many more questions face the minister's family. The answers largely depend on what we as mothers instill into their young lives, and also what we teach them in their growing-up years.

May we take it as a challenge! Living in a glass house is living an open and honest life each day. Then we can say with Joshua: "As for me and my house, we will serve the Lord" (Josh. 24:15b).

"If there is righteousness in the heart, then there is beauty in the character. If there is beauty in the character, then there is harmony in the family. If there is harmony in the family, there will be order in the nation. When there is order in the nation, then there is peace in the world." (Chinese proverb).

The Life That Counts

The life that counts must toil and fight;
Must hate the wrong and love the right,
Must stand for truth by day and night:
This is the life that counts.

The life that counts must aim to rise
Above the earth to sunlit skies;
Must fix its gaze on Paradise—
That is the life that counts.

The life that counts must helpful be;
In darkest night make melody;
Must wait the dawn on bended knee—
That is the life that counts.

The life that counts must helpful be;
The cares and needs of others see;
Must seek the slave of sin to free—
That is the life that counts.

A.W.S.

From A
Minister's Daughter
To A Minister's Wife

by Ruth (Mrs. James) Yoder

It all began on the evening of May 3, 1959, when God reached down and chose my earthly father as a minister to share the gospel of Jesus Christ to the poor; and to preach deliverance to the brokenhearted, and deliverance to the captives. It was a time never to be forgotten as his charge was so solemly given to heed the call as long as health and life shall last. Then the hearty, but sober, prayers of blessings went heaven-ward as the ministerial hands were placed on the heads of my father, mother, my three brothers, and myself. What an overwhelming experience! Then there were those tender handshakes and people wishing us the grace of God and telling us that they would be praying for us. What a consolation!

When all was over and people were leaving, we too gathered into the family car. I recall that we were indeed a sober crew as we headed for home. We all assured our dad that we'd do what we could to support him, and try to make his new calling in the ministry an easy and joyous one, if at all possible.

Even the very air that we breathed seemed to send forth a fragrance of peace and joy. I had an increased desire to obey God's voice in my own life, whatever the call might be.

It was the beginning of something new taking hold on my young life. Coming as a sweet scent from somewhere was the comforting realization that God could unfold the mystery of my future.

There was no long lapse in time before we discovered that the minister's family is privileged with many visitors. Some were prearranged, and many were surprise visitors. How very interesting! The Scripture term "given to hospitality" took on new meaning as food was prepared, or the bed sheets were changed for some more weary travelers, perhaps old friends, but also people we had never met before.

The work of the church was also a new chapter in my life. Little had I realized so soon after this touch of the Lord's hand upon us, we would be weighed down with burdens and cares we never had experienced before.

When Dad hurt, we all hurt. When he was burdened, we were all burdened. When he rejoiced, we all rejoiced. We were one team working for the same cause.

The time soon came when Dad was called to evangelistic work. That meant Dad could be gone for a week, two weeks, and even sometimes three. That was a great sacrifice on our part. However, not once did we doubt the wisdom of God to include the sharing of the Good News away from home. Jesus says, "Verily I say unto you, there is no man that hath left house, or brethren, or sisters, or father, or mother, or wife, or children, or lands, for my sake, and the gospel's, but he shall receive an hundredfold now in this time, houses, and brethren, and sisters, and mothers, and children, and lands, with persecutions; and in the world to come eternal life" (Mark 10:29, 30). In these times Mother and we children had many times of sharing and praying. Indeed, it was a special privilege to have part in the work of God's Kingdom.

There were times when we were all called together in one circle, and Dad would have something very important to say. Sometimes my flesh would not enjoy this type of gathering, because once again someone had suggested that the minister's children should live on a higher level than others, and we had not reached that level yet. Were we to be "super" children and not make mistakes? Were all the other children's and youth's activities to be different from the ones we participated in? That hurt. However, God's hand was again touching my life and was molding me for the future.

At other times we all rejoiced together in the same kind of circle, because some needy soul had found our Lord as Saviour. Those were the times when our spirits were lifted; and we knew God *does* have a purpose in a surrendered, though sometimes lonesome, life in the midst of a multitude of people.

As time and experience sped on, I met one whom God had also been molding and shaping for the future. His experience seemed to coincide with my own. It was no great surprise to me when he disclosed the news of his calling to the foreign field in the near future.

Could the life of a missionary's wife be comparable to the life of a minister's daughter? Is this perhaps what God was telling me back in May of 1959, when I was pondering over God's unfolding of the mystery of my future? My answer today is "Yes," but *this* is only the beginning.

Six weeks after we were married, we left for Berlin, Germany, where we served as missionaries for five years, September, 1963, to October, 1968.

We had the pleasure of living with a unit. My husband filled in to give topics in the absence of our minister, and also had many personal involvements in visitation and counseling.

Life had many trials in working with people, especially in a culture which we knew so little about. We praise God that the blessings far outweighed the frustrations. Looking back we can see, and say it truly was a preparing ground for what God had further planned for us. During this time we were blessed with two children, for which we were very grateful.

In October, 1968, we returned home. The "adjustments" were not easy, but as time goes on we find that adjustments are always a part of life.

In April, 1970, my husband was ordained to the ministry. Again a new chapter opened in our lives, in which we want to be faithful for God's glory. By this time we had another son added to our number. There were more challenges, more burdens, more trials—but also more blessings.

After several years in the ministry, my husband was called away from home to have meetings and was gone for one to two weeks at a time. Later he was involved in teaching at Calvary Bible School. Having small children and being alone in these times drew my thoughts back to the time when I was still at home as a minister's daughter, when my father was away from home; many times my mother had also gone with him.

As our children are growing up, they are facing the same struggles I had as a minister's child. It has been a help to me to share my experience with our children, and also to see *their* point of view.

The same is true in regard to standing for the principles of the Bible. Even though there are those among us who are losing convictions, it is our responsibility to keep on teaching and training without wavering as long as we live. Being a minister's wife is not something to be taken lightly. Frivolous living and giddy permissiveness would be a detriment to our calling. The teachings of our Lord need to be passed down from generation to generation until His soon return.

The years have rolled by, and God has continued to lead us through many struggles—and abundant blessings.

In September 1982, the Lord changed our position again when He called us to France to start a mission there. By this time we had another son, and an adopted daughter, bringing our number to five. Many contacts were made in this venture which added new friendships. Our children were at the age where we together faced some sad experiences, new challenges, and again more blessings. God, in His great mercy, taught us lessons of great value through it all. After three years we bade farewell again to the many more we had learned to love and appreciate, and returned home.

Little did we realize being at home only three years that God would call us to "move" so soon again. I am made aware that "I am not my own." God has called me to be a minister's wife. My earnest desire to Him is that He would help me to be faithful, and accept the call. If He desires that we "move again," may I be ready to go. "My grace is sufficient for thee" has been my theme.

We were asked to move to Belleville, Pennsylvania, which we did in March, 1989, where we are living at this writing.

God has been so good to us, and we know we are where God wants us to be now therefore, "we rejoice and are glad."

These years of being a minister's daughter, and now a minister's wife, have provided experiences I would not trade for anything else. They have been precious. Even though there have been some bitter experiences, God has a purpose in them all, and is still preparing me for the future when He will call me *Home* to *Himself.*

Some time after my husband's ordination a dear sister gave me a reading entitled, "So You are a Minister's Wife." These are some of the main points. 1. Be a good wife. 2. Be thankful. 3. Be a loving critic. 4. Be understanding. 5. Be confidential. 6. Be hospitable. 7. Be resigned. 8. Be devotional.

Dear ministers' wives, let us stand by our companions lest we be found wanting. We are in the work, building for eternity.

ᗰᘓ

About the Writer

James and Ruth grew up as minister's children, which helped to prepare them for their own ministry at home and abroad.

They are the parents of four children: Nathan and Martha, presently serving in Belize under Amish Mennonite Aid; Timothy and Linus, at home. They adopted Dorcas, a "special" child, who needs much supervision.

Ruth is kept busy with domestic duties and enjoys gardening and flowers as her hobbies. James is assisting in the ministry at the Pleasant View Church in Belleville, PA., and is a carpenter by trade.

If the Lord does not deliver
us out of trials,
He will go with us through them.

Spread It Before The Lord

Isaiah 37:14

Go, spread before the Lord thine empty barrel,
  Thy failing cruse of oil, thy slender purse;
He feedeth birds, gives flowers their rich apparel,
  And shall He see His children faring worse?

Go spread before the Lord that startling letter
  Which brings dismay or trouble to thy breast
Like one of old, prove that it is far better
  To throw its weight on Him, and be at rest.

Spread out before the Lord those sins besetting,
  That bring the blush of failure to thy face,
And fill thy heart with sorrowful regretting
  Christ giveth conquests in His secret place!

Spread out before the Lord that long-felt worry;
  Speak of it often to thy Heavenly Friend;
He that believeth shall not want to hurry
  Himself or God towards an unexpected end.

Spread out before the Lord from its beginning
  Each piece of work attempted for His sake;
Each call to service, social or soul-winning,
  No step at thine own charges thou must take.

Spread out before the Lord thy daily duty,
  It is not waste of time to tell Him all;
So shall life be "for glory and for beauty"
  If Jesus guides in greatest things and small.

—*Winifred A. Iverson*

Encouraging Your Minister Husband

by Edna (Mrs. Perry) Troyer

"The word of the Lord came unto me, saying, Before I formed thee in the belly I knew thee; and before thou camest forth out of the womb I sanctified thee, and I ordained thee a prophet unto the nations. Then said I, Ah, Lord God! Behold, I cannot speak; for I am a child. But the Lord said unto me, Say not, I am a child: for thou shalt go to all that I shall send thee, and whatsoever I command thee thou shalt speak. Be not afraid of their faces: for I am with thee to deliver thee, saith the Lord. Then the Lord put forth his hand, and touched my mouth. And the Lord said unto me, Behold, I have put my words in thy mouth. See, I have this day set thee over the nations and over the kingdoms, to root out, and to pull down, and to destroy, and to throw down, to build, and to plant" (Jer. 1:4-10).

It is important that we recognize that the call to the ministry is a divine call from God, and that we are willing to accept it as such. We are not our own, we are bought with a price. " I heard the voice of the Lord, saying, 'whom shall I send, and who will go for us?' Then said I, 'Here am I; send me' " (Isa. 6:8).

To encourage means to give confidence to; to inspire with courage, spirit, or strength of mind; to help; give support to; be favorable to; inspiring with hope and confidence.

How can we encourage our minister husband? First, we must allow God to search us, and to cleanse us from all that is impure; to be totally yielded to His call for each of us to be obedient to His voice, cheerfully to follow wherever He leads.

There are times when problems arise and it seems there is no immediate solution. We need to be strong and of good courage, waiting on the Lord. He is the answer to every problem. As wives, we must be encouragers. "Bear ye one another's burdens, and so fulfill the law of Christ" (Gal. 6:2). To let him know we care and stand by his side will spur him onward. "And let us not be weary in well doing: for in due season we shall reap if we faint not" (Gal. 6:9).

One may well faint if he expects to see the harvest immediately. "I have planted, Apollos watered; but God gave the increase. So then neither is he that planteth anything, neither he that watereth; but God that giveth the increase" (I Cor. 3:6, 7). "We are laborers together with God" (I Cor. 3:9).

In order for the wife to encourage her minister husband, she must have a close relationship with God and keep the lines of communication open between her and God, being sensitive to His still, small voice. We must also communicate as husband and wife. We must be worthy to receive clear insights from God.

I have become his wife, and do want to submit to him, obey and reverence him. Can I be like Sarah? She called Abraham "lord;" obeying, listening, following.

Am I tempted with self-pity, jealousy, worry, revenge? These are not the fruit of the Spirit. We do have our difficulties and some problems that those among the laity do not have. But God is our strength, a very present help in time of trouble. We recognize the sufficiency of God's grace.

Your minister husband may have been chosen because of strong conviction. Do I share all of these strong convictions? The church detects when there are strained relationships in the minister's home.

When we see that correction may be needed, we do so only in true love and in the right motive. Ask God for wisdom to tell it in a way he will accept and profit by it. Also let him know that you appreciated his message and that you were inspired by it.

We need to forget self in the pursuit of our husband's needs, and for those for whom he is responsible.

We need to be available when people need us. Listen, counsel, go! Listening involves hearing what is being said, and implied! We must always be approachable. Approach the impossible with confidence. Get down and cry unto God! He has what it takes. He IS the answer to all our needs. We work together with God. Let Him lead and enable us through these "impossible" situations. It creates confidence. Identify with each other's problems. Develop a heart of love, care and compassion for the people. Whatever you do, be kind.

Don't be defeated by mistakes. Learn from them. Most mistakes need not be final.

We can never share what isn't ours. Know the Word and its Author. Pray that God would not let us take our own way, but His way!

There are times when your minister husband is called away from home; for an evening, week-end meetings, a week of meetings, or whatever the occasion may be.

We must not be selfish, but willing to "let go" and

allow God to have His way in these decisions. There are times when it may be more appropriate for him to stay at home and fulfill his responsibility as father and head of the home, than to go. We dare not neglect our own family. But as wife and children, we can be richly blessed to allow and encourage him to go whenever God so desires.

"He must be one who manages his own household well, keeping his children under control with all dignity, (but if a man does not know how to manage his own household, how will he take care of the church of God?) . . . Women must likewise be dignified, not malicious gossips, but temperate, faithful in all things" (I Tim. 3:4, 5, 11, Discovery Bible).

"Ye are bought with a price: therefore glorify God in your body, and in your spirit, which are God's . . . be not ye the servants of men" (I Cor. 6:20, 7:23). "Hereby perceive we the love of God, because he laid down his life for us; and we ought to lay down our lives for the brethren" (I Jn. 3:16). Here, in a few words, we are reminded of our supreme duty to God and the church. In loyal, willing, self-sacrificing, wholehearted service, without any reservations of a world-compromising nature, our lives should be placed upon the altar, in which case God can use the whole powers of our being to the glory of His name and the advancement of His cause.

Numerous instances are recorded in the Word where the cause of Christ and the church was strengthened through prayer. Witness, for instance, the apostolic company in the upper room in Jerusalem previous to the outpouring of the Holy Ghost on the day of Pentecost (Acts 1:13-2:4); the disciples in the home of Mary praying for Peter (Acts 12;5, 12); the praying church at Antioch just before sending forth Paul and Barnabas as missionaries to the Gentiles (Acts 13:1-4); and numerous other occasions where prayer was resorted to with great faith and power. We need not be seriously alarmed about any church whose membership is given to much fervent, sincere and intelligent praying.

As ministers' wives, we dare not neglect the intercessory prayer for God's direction—not only for the messages across the pulpit, but in every phase of our lives. Only as God directs and inspires by the Holy Spirit can the seed go forth and bear fruit to His praise and glory. We see the importance of being careful to give God all praise and glory for any and all good that comes through the vessel.

Moses praying on the hill may remind us of Christ in heaven interceding for His church on earth. Moses interceded, while holding up in his hands the rod of God (Exodus 17: 9, 11). The rod was the symbol of God's power as pledged for the defense of Israel. Faith holds up the rod in laying hold on God's word and promise, and pleading the same before Him. Moses had able coadjutors. Aaron and Hur stayed up his hands when they grew heavy through fatigue (v. 12). Here we may apply the wife and children as being the coadjutors—or those who aid and assist their husband and father. It is a happy circumstance when those who bear the principal burden of responsibility in spiritual work can rely on being aided by the sympathy and cooperation of others, "like-minded" (Phil. 2:20) with themselves in their desire to see God's kingdom making progress. God's people hold up the hands of ministers by praying for them (I Thess. 5:25). Would that the church were more alive to this secret of gaining victories by earnest supplication! The influence of prayer cannot be overrated. It decides battles. It opens and shuts the windows of heaven (James 5:17, 18).

At our husband's ordination we sisters promised to accept our husband's call as from God, and that we would support him. I like what the Ministers' Manual has to say about the Minister's Wife: "The sister whose husband is in the ministry has a very important role in the work of the church.

"The faithful wife is clothed with meekness and quietness. She is of a submissive spirit, obedient to her husband. Her life will enhance his acceptability and usefulness. She is an example for all women in all things. As a rare jewel, she ornaments the work of her husband.

"She shall visit, comfort, and take care of the poor, the weak, the afflicted, and the needy, as well as the orphans and widows.

"Furthermore, she shall help her husband to carry out his duties in the church in ways that are properly in her sphere.

"She will arrange her schedules to accommodate her husband in his preaching, visitation, work, and study schedule.

"Her house is in such order so as to accommodate visitors and guests at any time. As they share together the burden of their home and the church, she becomes a wise counselor to her husband. She helps him maintain propriety in his conduct and stability in his work.

'She is not a 'busybody in other men's matters' but a 'keeper at home.' She is, however, interested in others, seeing their needs and reaching out under the direction of her husband to meet those needs. She shall edify and instruct other women, especially those younger, counseling women and girls in their particular needs. She is not a gossiper. (Titus 2:3-5).

"The minister is to keep his children in subjection. He

and his wife will stand together in relation to training, discipline, admonishing, and in instructing.

"The wife will always support her faithful husband in his work. When he is misunderstood or not appreciated, she becomes an understanding and comforting companion.

"She is a faithful example in obedience to the church standards and discipline, and with her husband maintains a vibrant, living relationship with the Lord through personal communion with God. The Word and thy Holy Spirit are her very real companions. The incense of her prayer is constantly rising to heaven, thus blessing the home, the church, and the community at large."

It takes the daily presence of God to fulfill our responsibilities.

〰

Perry and Edna have been lifelong residents at Plain City, Ohio. They have three children.

Their family has been a real blessing and contribution to the Bethesda church and the surrounding communities for many years.

Perry served as deacon for 9 years. He was ordained bishop of the church in March of 1987.

He is also a board member of the Mission Interest Committee. They do some extensive traveling to visit missions in the far North and in Europe.

The Troyers live on a small farm. Perry is a carpenter by trade and Edna is a homemaker and has the gift of sharing wherever there is a need.

Constancy

It is something sweet, when the world goes ill,
To know you are faithful and love me still;
To feel when the sunshine has left the skies,
That the light is shining in your dear eyes;
Beautiful eyes, more dear to me
Then all the wealth of the world could be.

It is something, dearest, to feel you near,
When life with its sorrows seems hard to bear;
To feel, when I falter, the clasp divine
Of your tender and trusting hand in mine;
Beautiful hand, more dear to me
Than the tenderest thing on earth could be.

Sometimes, dearest, the world goes wrong,
For God gives grief with His gift of song,
And poverty, too, but your love is more
To me than riches and golden store;
Beautiful Love, until death shall part,
It is mine—as you are—my own sweetheart!

—*Frank L. Stanton*

Communication
(Between the Minister and His Wife)
by Ruth (Mrs. John H., Jr.) Miller

C ommunication is one of the greatest tests in the normal home. A normal home that is struggling to survive in today's world with the added stress of Daddy being a preacher, is even a greater test.

The hour-long telephone conversations that can be explained in five minutes; the late night meeting that brings husband home too tired to talk; the counseling session which must be kept confidential (and I do want it that way); the unexplained change in plans at the last minute because someone needed the security of his deacon's counsel; these are all a part of a normal deacon's home.

Those weeks and weekends when Daddy is gone, the responsibility of guiding the family rests more heavily on Mother's shoulders. She answers the many questions of the toddler, becomes a sounding board for the adolescent, a buffer for the teenager, and an advisor to the young adult, while thinking over and over, "If only Daddy were here, everything would be all right." These all add to the normalcy of the deacon's home.

Because of such situations, we could fail the test of

communication in our marriage; but praise God, He doesn't ask us to take this test by ourselves. God promises His grace for us as each new day arrives. Let us not borrow tomorrow's trouble against today's grace! I shall never forget my mother's advice to me as a teenager, "Take life one day at a time." (Thanks, Mom!)

I'm so thankful our marriage need not barely exist, or just survive. If I am willing to expend the energy and take the time to communicate and transmit my innermost feelings of love and appreciation for my deacon husband, then communication can flourish and soar to heights of majestic bliss. This can only be accomplished if I first have a deep and abiding relationship with my heavenly Father who has the answers to all our problems. (Thank You, God!)

So, when do I look deeply into the soul of the one to whom I have betrothed my very life? Time is so elusive. When we have grown older, we may find that we wish we could have somehow been able to bottle and save it. But that is not possible, so we must do next best; we have to take the time now!

Traveling is probably our favorite time spent together. Going "home" at Christmas time is always special. (We live in Ohio and Daddy's home is in Virginia.) We often travel at night. The children usually fall asleep soon after our midnight snack. We have munchies and coffee along, which last for hours. As we travel my husband and I eat together, sing together, and talk together all night long. The phone doesn't ring, and there are no emergency service calls to disrupt our communication. (My deacon husband is also a plumber.) NO, it's just the traffic, my God, my husband, and myself.

We've solved many problems, worked our way through

personal differences, and shared ideals, aspirations, goals for our children, as well as hopes for the future, on the road. God seems especially close on such trips together. These times become our "oases;" our shock absorber for the turbulent days ahead. They help me cope with the buffeting winds of turmoil which I sometimes encounter along life's way. They help me head into the wind with my head down, knowing that this too shall pass, and God's grace is there for this day also.

I must show my love and my loyalty to my husband in every situation. Especially does he need this assurance during trying times of his ministry when it seems most people misunderstand the stand he is taking along with his fellow ministers. He needs to sense my support at this time, and that I believe in and trust his judgment. He should never have to walk this road without me.

There was a time in my life when I thought I could disengage myself from my husband's ministry and still remain in the will of God. (God, forgive me!) How could I have been so selfish? I deeply regret this time in my life. It was such a dark valley I tried to walk through alone. This valley grew darker and the night became longer as I nearly destroyed that beautiful communion I had with my husband. But God was merciful to me and drew me to Himself; took my hand and guided me once again into the path where He wanted me to walk. The peace that was mine as I yielded myself to God was so very precious. I know God is not finished gently nudging me with His Spirit. May I always be sensitive to His touch.

I need to communicate my submission to God's order in our home, so that beyond the shadow of a doubt, my husband will be able to trust me while he is gone. Is he able to trust me to make decisions and guide our home in such a manner that he does not have to worry or be ashamed? It is important that our children realize that rules do not change because Daddy is gone. Life goes on as if Daddy were still at the helm. Actually he is, only he doesn't happen to be on site at the moment. His influence goes on. The training, the teaching, the time he has invested with the children; these things surface in many ways even while he is not here. I want to be sure Daddy realizes this, so that his mind can be at rest about things at home, and the Spirit of God be not hindered in any way. He needs to be able to focus totally on the responsibilities before him.

It is always a happy day when Daddy is due home or when we go to meet him at the end of week-long revival meetings. I'll never forget the Sunday morning when I took our six children in the car, and equipped with donuts, orange juice, coffee, several changes of clothes in case of spills, books to read and lots of patience, we started at 4:30 A.M. for Belleville, Pennsylvania. It was a perfect morning and there was very little traffic. There was only the hum of our own tires as our headlights played out across the long expanse of highway that stretched endlessly into the darkness of the early morning. Everyone was so happy. We sang and laughed as we told stories for the first hour or so. My heart was so full of happiness and joy that I thought it would burst!

God had wonderfully brought us through a week of being at home while Daddy was away preaching and everyone had weathered the week well. I could feel the presence of God in such a real way throughout the week. Now we were on our way to see Daddy and to show him our love and support. We wanted him to know that we believe in him, and we wanted to hear him preach the Word of God. (My husband is also my favorite preacher.)

We arrived at the church in time for the morning message. The smile that stretched on and on when he stood up to preach was well worth the effort it took to get there. (So was the hug he gave me standing in the aisle afterwards!)

I want our home to be a haven for my husband to come home to; a place where peace and tranquility abide, a place where he feels love and acceptance, not just from me, his wife, but from his whole family. I want our children to rise up and call him blessed.

About The Writer

Since their marriage, March 30, 1964, John and Ruth have resided in Minerva, Ohio. John is a plumbing and heating contractor and Ruth is seen as a cheerful wife and mother of six children.

John was ordained deacon on January 30, 1983, and has also been faithful in proclaiming God's Word in evangelistic work. Ruth's hobbies are reading, sewing, and walking.

Requirements For Contented Living

1. Health enough
   to make work a pleasure.
2. Wealth enough
   to support your needs.
3. Strength enough
   to battle with difficulties
     and overcome them.
4. Patience enough
   to toil until some good is accomplished.
5. Grace enough
   to confess your sins and forsake them.
6. Charity enough
   to see some good in your neighbor.
7. Love enough
   to move you to be useful to others.
8. Faith enough
   to make real the things of God.
9. Hope enough
   to remove anxious fears for the future.

—*Papyrus*

Living On A Pastor's Salary

by Lavina (Mrs. Elmer) Gingerich

My minister husband was scheduled to leave for a week of meetings the day our chicken check arrived in the mail. Expecting the usual average amount, we felt momentarily shocked to find the amount to be only half of what we had anticipated.

With a feeling of numbness within ourselves, we simply dropped to our knees and committed our finances to the Lord that morning. Our Heavenly Father comforted us with a strange mixture of submission, sadness, and joy in our hearts that the world knows nothing of.

Somehow that experience was just what we needed before my husband left for those meetings. It made us keenly aware that we dare not trust in our own abilities. No matter how "good" we may be at chicken growing or preaching, it is God who controls our income, or the success of preaching!

Finances are a real part of life for each of us including minister families. It does take money to live, and it is scriptural to provide for our own household. However, it is definitely unscriptural to love money and the things of this world that money will buy. Jesus never condemned money or possessions in themselves, but He had much to say about our attitude toward them.

Minister families should be examples of faithfulness in money matters. Jesus said in Luke 16:11, "If therefore ye have not been faithful in the unrighteous mammon [money], who will commit to your trust the true riches?" It is sobering to think that God will test our readiness to receive and use spiritual riches by how responsible we are with money.

Whether or not a person operates from a servant's heart or practices self-discipline probably shows up in money matters more than any other area. The measure of our faithfulness is evidenced in our attitude toward debt, our policy to drive bargains, our insistence of the best prices for our products, and in general, by how we are controlled by the dollar.

God usually gives us direction regarding a purchase by whether we have the money or not. He knows what is best for us and will protect us from making unnecessary or harmful purchases. If we lack the funds, it may well be that we don't really need it.

At one point in our lives, it was becoming more and more of a common experience for our family to get into a financial bind just prior to the arrival of the chicken check. It was my husband's suggestion (more than once) that we should make out a weekly budget and stick to it. My heart rebelled at the idea! I actually felt hurt, because I thought I had tried to be saving and as thrifty as I knew how to be. Now I was being asked to budget our income even closer. But I didn't really understand what living on a budget would mean.

At first I felt frustrated when I went to town knowing there was only a certain amount of money allotted for that week's needs. To my amazement there was usually money left over at the end of the week. And what a feeling of security to know there would be money for each week until the chicken check would come again! I was experiencing a new freedom and it was naturally a strength to our marriage relationship to have the atmosphere free from tension caused by money problems.

Our income actually continued to be much the same as it had been before, but we had learned that we do spend more when we think we have more. Although we were driven to do this out of necessity, it has become our conviction that Christians should budget their money out of a desire to follow scriptural principles of stewardship.

A pastor's wife will often need to ask herself, "Which is of more value, a trip to minister to hungry souls, or making money at home? And then there are the many, sometimes lengthy, long distance telephone calls concerning church work, listening to someone's problems, etc. There are also those times when your pastor husband will need to forfeit working hours to spend time in preparation for a message or writing a letter or other ministerial responsibilities.

It's at these times that we face the test of what is most valuable to us, money or souls? It is good to remember that when our earthly life is over, the only thing we can take with us is our children or other souls. Even if we're able to keep our earthly possessions for which we have worked so hard for many years, they are not eternal!

Pressure, which originated in the world, is now increasing among mothers in the church to work outside of the home. Whether it is a result of peer pressure to keep up with others financially or a lack of fulfillment in staying at home with the family, it does not seem scriptural. God designed a wife to find her fulfillment by being a "help meet" to her husband (Gen. 2:18).

Parents often find it necessary to use available resources in designing products in their home or on their farm to provide work for their growing children. Even then, we need to check our motives regularly. Is doing this strengthening our marriage or endangering it? Is it bringing glory to God? Titus 2:5 encourages older women to teach the young women to be "keepers at home" that the Word of God be not blasphemed. Is is extending my husband's ministry or bringing reproach to it? In I Tim. 5:14 the younger women are admonished to "marry, to bear children, guide the house, give none occasion to the adversary to speak reproachfully."

It is so important to keep our focus on right values. Which has the most eternal value—being available when they need us or being able to buy more *things* for the family? May we find our fulfillment in being keepers at home, making it a pleasant (though perhaps simple) refuge that husband and children love to come home to!

Although the husband should rightfully be the financial leader in the home, a wife can certainly help relieve some of the pressures involved.

The following are some practical suggestions to help reduce financial distress in our homes:

1. Purpose to be submissive to your husband's leadership in money matters. Help him work out a budget and experience the security of living within that budget.
2. Enjoy the possessions that God has entrusted to you and avoid comparing your things with someone else's. Develop a grateful spirit for everything from your groceries to your furniture and clothing.
3. Avoid window shopping. Someone has suggested that this is an exercise of discontentment.
4. When you are debating about whether to buy an item or

not, test yourself with this question. "Will I be eager to tell my husband about my purchase?"

5. Be sure to check the price tag before you examine the product and get your heart set on it. Satan always wants us to focus on the pleasure of sin rather than the cost of it!

6. Invest time in teaching and training your sons and daughters to become creative and thrifty in homemaking skills.

7. Keep in mind that the easiest way to gain financial freedom is not to increase your income but to decrease your bills, and wives can do much to accomplish this.

8. Learn to sift your wants from your needs. We may believe and trust that "God shall supply all your needs according to his riches in glory by Christ Jesus" (Phil. 4:19).

୧ﾉ𝕯

About the Writer

In their growing up years, both Elmer and Lavina lived in the Indiana-Michigan area.

They were married in March, 1964, and four years later they left the comforts of their home and a well-established church-life to pioneer a small mission outreach in the hills of Arkansas. Elmer was ordained minister in 1970 and eight years later he was ordained bishop of the Shady Lawn Church in Mt. View, Arkansas.

The Gingerich family consists of six children and they live on a poultry farm. Besides, they are involved in the Christian Day School where Elmer and two of their daughters have taught. Lavina keeps the home fires burning. She is also editor of the "Home Maker's Hints" and the Junior Department in the Calvary Messenger.

Ten Tips For Coping With Stress

1. Begin the day with God. Read His word, talk to Him in prayer. Rest in the Lord.
2. Take time to smell the flowers, listen to the birds chirp and sing. Visit a shut-in or write a letter.
3. Listen when others talk, doing only one thing at a time.
4. Drop annoying, time-consuming activities and obligations—things that have no eternal value.
5. Be open to share feelings of joy, grief, frustrations or disappointments, but recognize that each situation is allowed by God.
6. Stop trying to remember everything. Write things down, make notes of reminder for yourself.
7. Allow more time than you think you need to meet appointments, or go get a certain job done. Allow time for the unexpected.
8. Be prepared to wait. Keep a small Bible, book or letter writing material in your purse so that you can make good use of moments while you wait.
9. Rid your life of clutter. If you haven't worn it or used it for a year, give it to someone who will use it.
10. Plan tomorrow before the end of the day. But keep in mind that plans are subject to change if God wills.

—*Selected & adapted by AMB*

Problem People Or People With Problems?
(My Husband's Companion)
by Pauline (Mrs. Simon) Schrock

P roblem people—Who are they? What are they like?
1. They are people with inner needs.
2. They are people who need to be heard, and who need to experience sympathy from another.
3. They are people for whom Christ died.
4. They are people worth trying to understand.

What is a companion?
- One who stands by.
- One he can trust.
- Someone he can talk to and know it will not be passed on.
- One he knows will lift him up in prayer as he goes.

Am I a companion? Or am I so time-centered and organized that I cannot leave something undone in order to spend time in prayer for my husband when the need arises, or a call comes to counsel someone? What if I have a special supper planned or something special with the family, and someone calls to talk with or meet with my husband, because he needs to talk? What is my response? Am I a companion? What does my attitude say to the children?

113

After receiving this writing assignment, it seemed I had a lot of learning to do, searching my life for right attitudes and feelings toward people. It was one case right after the other; one week my husband was gone almost every evening. Sometimes Satan tempts us, hoping we'll fall; God tests us, hoping we'll grow! I thank God that He tests me in areas where I need to grow and lean heavily on Him!

As a companion, am I willing to operate flexibly enough to plunge into unplanned situations that arise, or when my husband needs prayer support from a companion? He cultivates seeing people for what they can become in Christ, not just for what they are. His goal is to draw out the best, encourage the good, nudge them on to growth and victory.

As he goes, do I really carry the same concern? Do I give him a look of love and sharing concern, or a look of "Oh no, not again!"? I believe my attitude toward the person or problem, and toward his leaving has a lot to do with how he can respond to the person and problem.

We have gone on a number of camping trips in the past. In the evening we enjoyed sitting around the campfire. Often when we went to bed there would be a pile of red ashes. In the morning someone would stir the coals. If there were still red embers, the challenge was to blow and gently fan the spark that may start a fire. Small sticks would be placed on the embers, and then fanned till they burst into a little flame. Then larger wood was placed on the fire, and soon everyone could enjoy the warmth of the fire.

As a companion, I need to see that spark of hope in the other person, and fan the spark into flame. Husband and wife together, must see it as an opportunity and not as a nuisance.

It is rewarding when you see people change, and together we can praise and thank God. One person with whom he worked, and to whom he continued to write notes occasionally, called my husband when he accepted Christ and said, "I want to tell you first that I accepted Christ." There are rewards!

As a companion, how do I or should I respond when there are problems, and he is under so much pressure and tension that he is not his normal self toward his wife or children? Do I get uptight, too? Or am I willing to carry a little more of the load, keeping things running a little more smoothly with the children at that time? Do I spend enough time in prayer for him?

I feel that when he is under pressure is the time the children and I need to stand by him, and let him know that we really care, sharing his concern and praying for him. At such a time we need to be patient, longsuffering, and giving love. We need to help the children understand, so they also pray for Dad.

My attitude at such a time, will have an effect on how the children accept and feel about their dad being in the ministry. We don't need to tell them what the problem is, but to pray for strength and wisdom for Dad.

As a companion, do I really listen to what he has to say, or do I jump to a conclusion about the problem before I have really listened to what he has to say and is feeling?

What is the best way to encourage my husband at such a time? I can leave him a note on his desk, or in his Bible, or something I find helpful in my private devotions. Just sharing simple little notes can mean a lot to him. We need to always keep communications open, especially during times of tension and pressure.

A rose is a beautiful flower, but it also has thorns. Do

we focus on the beauty of the flower, or on the thorns? Depending what we focus on, it makes a big difference whether we appreciate the flower or not. My prayer is that I may see each person as a rose, and focus on what they can become in Christ. If I focus on the thorns, or the hurt, and keep harboring on that, it would cause me to feel bitter toward that person. I could not really support my husband with that kind of feeling. Frances J. Roberts says:

> "Look not on thine own thoughts, but walk in the Spirit: so shalt thou accomplish the work which the Spirit desireth to do. Eternity alone shall reveal the fruit of this hidden ministry. For we labor not in this material realm, and we work not with the elements of this world; but our labor is in the realm of the Spirit, and the accomplishments are not judged by the human eye, but shall be revealed in the light of eternity.
>
> "Therefore be diligent. Follow me so closely that there shall be no distance between. Listen carefully to My voice, that thou go not thine own way. For My path shineth more and more brightly unto that day. Set thine heart to follow to the end, for at the end there is laid up an exceeding weight of glory for them that endure."[1]

Allen Loy McGinnis says:

> "When we get discouraged in our work with people, it is important to draw back and remind ourselves that there is no more noble occupation in

---

1. Frances J. Roberts, *Come Away My Beloved,* King's Farspan, Inc.

the world than to assist another human being, to help someone else succeed."[2]

If I keep this in focus, it will help me to be a better companion to my husband as he works and counsels with people.

Here are some contributions I can make in promoting the principle of using hospitality one to another:

- My husband appreciates when I show an interest in the people who are seeking help.
- He appreciates when I am friendly with those with whom we need to counsel.
- He appreciates when I show hospitality to people, and especially those considered to be problem people.
- He appreciates when I prepare refreshments to share with people who come by to talk.
- He appreciates when we can show love and care by sharing with those we need to counsel and admonish.

PRAYER: Lord, help me to be a faithful companion to my husband, to stand by him, encourage him, and lift him daily to Your throne in prayer.

❧

About the Writer

Simon and Pauline Schrock are living at 4614 Holly Ave., Fairfax, Va. They were married September 29, 1963. October 30, 1977 he was ordained to the ministry, and August 30, 1981, to the office of bishop. They are blessed with three children.

2. Source of quote unknown.

Their family is greatly appreciated for their untiring faithfulness at Faith Christian Fellowship, Catlett, Va., and also in the community. They take time to listen, when someone needs to talk. Brother Schrock is president of Choice Books of Northern Virginia, which has almost 1400 book racks along the East Coast. He is a contributing editor to *Calvary Messenger* and has written several books, including *One Anothering, Get On With Living,* and *Vow-Keepers, Vow-Breakers.* Their children also help in the office and are a blessing to their parents' ministry.

Compassion is the capacity to put love into action.

Do It Now

It seems we have so little time
        To do the kindly things;
Before we realize the truth,
        We find that time has wings.

We plan to give a word of cheer
        To one who needs a friend;
We plan to see someone who's ill,
        Who may be near the end.

And there's a letter we should write
        To someone who is sad;
Our word may be just what they need
        To cheer and make them glad.

It's easy to procrastinate
        And leave such tasks undone,
But such a course will bring regrets
        When life's short race is run.

There is a cure for all these ills:
        Just three words tell us how
To bring a speedy, perfect cure;
        They're simply "Do it Now."

—*Author Unknown*

Feeling With People Who Hurt

by Anna Mary (Mrs. Bennie) Byler

Life is filled with sorrow and care
Days are lonely and drear
Burdens are lifted at Calvary
Jesus is very near!

A s I think of a world full of people who hurt, my mind goes to this song.

All around us are people who know what sorrow is all about, and everywhere there are people who are groping for something. Blessed are those who know that burdens are lifted at Calvary. But that is not enough!

There was the little child who was afraid during a storm. When told that God was there, the child responded by saying, "Yes, but I want someone with skin on." Isn't that how it is today in this hurting world? We all know that burdens are lifted at Calvary, and that Jesus is very near, but we also need to have those who care and know what the hurt is all about. ". . . and I sat where they sat" (Ezekiel 3:15b). If we feel with those who hurt, we must be a part of their hurt.

How often do you pray, "Make me sensitive today,"

121

and yet go right on living for self, thinking, "tomorrow I'll write that letter; tomorrow I will spend more time praying for those in need; or perhaps next week I'll take supper in for the sick neighbor."

Yes, we ask God to make us sensitive; yet we put it off for a more "convenient" time, or think that another sister in the church has so much more time. She has no little ones to care for, her house is always in order, she is more qualified . . . on and on . . . yet all around us are those who need that word of encouragement now! They need that letter now, or that prayer now!

Really, where are our priorities? Are they achieving for self, or are we more concerned that God's will be done?

For a moment, let us picture ourselves being the one who has just experienced an accident hundreds of miles from home. The husband is pronounced dead soon after being taken by helicopter to a more equipped, modern hospital, a daughter is killed instantly, and a teenaged son is just a breath away from eternity. Around you are four crying preschool children, frightened, bruised, and hurting, and a little daughter with a badly broken leg. Here you are, trying desperately to reach a familiar voice by phone, by which to ease this sudden, crushing, shocking feeling of being all alone.

Another glimpse takes us to a middle-aged wife looking out a window of an eleven-story hospital with only a purse and Bible in hand. Her husband had become suddenly ill while hundreds of miles from home. He had been busy with church work, and at an early morning hour found emergency surgery to be his lot. They are miles from home and feel all alone, needing desperately to reach someone who cares.

Then there were parents sitting beside a very sick

child's hospital bed . . . and numerous tubes, with groans being the only sounds that are heard; too sick for words, too sad for proper comprehension.

An aged couple is sitting in their room, hour after hour, day after day, wondering, "Why am I still here?" Their hearts are longing for the days when they could be useful in cracking nuts for the neighbors, hoeing thistles in the field, going for the mail, shelling peas and beans. But life for them is made of long, ticking hours, with no more goals to reach.

A widow is seen sitting on her rocking chair watching the family members busily hurrying about. Her days are long and lonely after caring for her husband nearly three years. She suddenly finds herself all alone, sitting with nothing to do, but hearing the noises and unfamiliar sounds of her well-kept house.

Another older lady is seen in a quiet little house, having cared for her sick husband twenty months, and meeting the demands of a strict schedule, she suddenly finds herself alone to care for a retarded son and a sick daughter. No husband to share with, no husband to encourage her . . . .

A young mother can be seen watching the window for approaching headlights . . . only to see them disappear again. Yes, she's left alone to answer those hard questions that the innocent ones ask. "Why isn't Daddy coming home? Why did he leave? I guess I'll just have God for my Daddy, if my daddy doesn't love us."

A very young mother wakes up to hear the doctor mention the word "Mongoloid." Another mother of her first child stands in front of the hospital nursery window observing the babies and notices her baby looks "different."

Yes, we are living in a hurting world, and all of us know. Yet, at times we need to be reminded that our burdens truly are lifted at Calvary. Nevertheless we, like the little child, need to also know that someone "with skin on" is close and does understand!

Many couples in different stages of life meet crises and sometimes feel "up against a wall." What an encouragement when a minister's wife, in the course of a conversation, shares that she and her husband also experienced such frustrations; but there is a way out. By sharing, both their burdens were lifted; and the wall which the couple thought was there could be "talked through."

There are hundreds of children and teenagers who are hurting because they were not prayed into the world. Many are abused and seemingly have life-long scars because of their hurt.

Then there are those who we meet in town who are seraching for "The Way," and in our hurry for material pursuit we fail to give them a word, or share our testimony. Perhaps we are even too engrossed with ourselves to notice their need of a smile.

A wedding causes much excitement. Families and friends look forward to the event with eager anticipation. The couple is showered with good wishes, but before the last echoes of congratulations have died away, the newly married couple is swept into the turbulent sea of marital adjustments, unnoticed by many.

The aftermath of a house or barn fire is a whirl of volunteer labor, many gifts of food, furnishings, words of comfort and expressions of concern that bring courage to those hurting. In short order the rubbish is cleaned and the new structure takes shape because many hands make the load light. Then the interest of the community wanes, leaving the family alone in their struggle to finish the many "loose ends." Long after the experience has been forgotten by neighbors and friends, these individuals still battle with nightmares and fear of yet another fire.

A sudden death, and especially someone of a young age, brings in its wake many concerned people. The entire community is bound by a feeling of shock and grief. Willing hands attend to details in preparation for the funeral, words and messages of sympathy flow from relatives and friends to comfort the sorrowing. But with time the concern fades, the mourning family moves from a cushioned state of shock to the realization of raw facts. Their coping has only begun when the support of others is already removed. How very important in a time like this for someone to just drop in and become the family's listening ear, especially when it's one of the parents who have been called home. To a teenager and even an adolescent's hurting heart, there is no better medicine then to know that someone cares enough to keep on showing interest.

In many circumstances such as these mentioned, a strong current of deep feeling sweeps through the persons and community involved; fervent prayers, volunteer labor and messages of sympathetic understanding are abundantly offered. Such immediate, genuine help is necessary, but more is needed. Too often support is withdrawn before the raw facts of life surface in stark reality. The problem is rooted in self-centeredness. We can show genuine compassion briefly, but when the novelty of the experience begins to fade, we revert to our own petty cares. We magnify our trivial problems and pursuits, allowing them to overshadow our concern for others. We ignore the importance of producing fruit of compassion as the Bible commands us to: "Bear ye one another's burdens," and "Weep with them that weep." Our self-centeredness deprives sufferers of the continual loving support *so* vital to them.

We must be more compassionate! We need to shift our gaze away from ourselves to become more thoroughly acquainted with the struggles of our fellow men. Although we can never realize the full extent of the difficulty other people face, we should strive to see it from their perspective. Only when we learn to walk in another's shoes can we produce the enduring fruit of genuine compassion. Ezekiel 3:15b, reminds us to "sit where they sit . . ." Let us become more sensitive and heed those still small probings. When we feel we should pray for someone, write a letter, or even make a phone call, let us be diligent to do it now! It may lift someone's spirits!

If our lives are in tune with God, then God's spirit is at work and we will be able by His grace to minister to those who hurt, even in the midst of our busy schedule, our growing family, or our added responsibility. God can be glorified by us responding to those who hurt.

In the first account, God's angels ministered to the mother's needs by providing hospital facilities to assist her in caring for her children. A physician called for volunteers; and people helped in three hour shifts, each bringing toys, books, and food. One nurse offered to do the laundry; community women arrived "just to be there," until the closest Mennonite community could be contacted. A Mennonite couple did go and comfort the sorrowing mother until her family arrived.

In the second account, friends were standing by. After contacting the home church, the people prayed, and God blessed the surgery beyond all expectation. Now after more than seven years the minister husband has completely recovered and is rejoicing in God's healing power.

Just being there, a phone call, an arrangement of flowers, words of encouragement, a hand clasp, visits, gifts of food, and money are all ways that help lighten the load in a trying experience.

In the account of the sick child a minister's visit revealed to him how deathly sick the child was, and prayers ascended to the Throne. God again answered the prayers, and the child was marvelously healed. The church was also strengthened and brought close together; again, helping each other see the need of the brotherhood.

When God brings a person to mind, let us not push the thought away, but breathe a prayer. If you feel the need of encouraging a brother or sister, do it. Give them a word or a letter. It takes so little time, yet means so much. Little do we know the struggle a person may be experiencing. And as we are sensitive to our heavenly Father's bidding, the letter or a word of encouragement may come at "just the right time." This also in turn is an encouragement to the sender to be yet more sensitive.

What about the lonely or aged neighbor? When we as mothers bake a pie, why not fill a small pie pan and share it with them? The reward of seeing their faces light up even brightens the life of the giver. Take in a meal for a busy family, perhaps someone who is caring for their aged parents. Give the family a break by staying with the aged person so the family can enjoy a refreshing ride on the mountain, or share with them some money so they can enjoy a good meal at a moderate restaurant where they are served and where the family ties are refreshed and renewed. Giving a listening ear to single friends who have no one to talk to, or inviting them to share an evening with the family, could lessen their hurt and lonely feelings.

The Bible also has something to share concerning the

need of comfort to a hurting world. "Who comforteth us in all our tribulation, that we may be able to comfort . . ." II Cor. 1:4. We must first be comforted by God, filled with His word and sensitive to His bidding in order to be able to share and comfort those who hurt.

Verse nine reminds us ". . . not to trust in ourselves, but in God which raiseth the dead." As we trust in God, the giver of all comfort, we will also respond to the needs of those around us.

The person who takes
time for prayer
will find time for all
the other things
needing his attention.

Giving

It's not what you get, but what you give,
That makes worthwhile the Life you live;
The transient thrill of receiving is gone,
While the joy of giving goes on and on;
For when you've performed a kindly deed,
Healed a hurt or supplied a need,
Deep in your heart there begins to glow
A warmth of gladness it's good to know!
You love the world! It loves you, too!
You smile, and it smiles right back at you;
And you say to yourself, "It's good to live!"
But, better still, when you've learned to give.

—*Thelma Williamson*

Born For Charity Work

by Anna Mary (Mrs. Bennie) Byler

"The work is solemn—therefore don't trifle;
The task is difficult—therefore don't relax;
The opportunity is brief—therefore don't delay;
The path is narrow—therefore don't wander;
The prize is glorious—therefore don't faint!"
—*D.M. Panton*

D o we not tend to bargain with God for this bottom line? "Lord, do I have to?" "How much must I give?" "Is it really required?"

Time, friends, family, money, and our own selves are all subject to Christian service. Any of us can raise the foregoing questions as we seek God's will in prayer. However, we must never seek answers different than those already given in the Scripture. Christian sacrifice is thoroughly dealt with in God's Word, and no sacrifice is too much!

In Luke 14:33 we are reminded that "whosoever he be of you that forsaketh not all that he hath, he cannot be my disciple." In Romans 12:1, we read that we must "present our bodies a living sacrifice."

"How much?" "Do we have to?" The answer is clearly

ALL! Everything! No cost too great; no service too much. God never asks for anything that He Himself doesn't already own, even though we may claim it possessively. The extent of our service leaves no question at all to be decided!

No sacrifice is too great, no call too demanding, no service too insignificant to the true disciple—the one who has already left all.

"He which soweth sparingly shall reap also sparingly; and he which soweth bountifully shall reap also bountifully. Every man according as he purposeth in his heart, so let him give; not grudgingly . . ." (II Cor. 9:6, 7).

These words state clearly how God wants us to respond to the great work that He has called all of His children to do. If we choose to be stingy, that is exactly how our reaping will be. If from a heartfelt love for our Creator and Maker we respond willingly and gladly, then our harvest will be one of blessings in this life and much more in the everlasting life to come.

Someone has said, "Serving with the right attitude makes duty a delight, not a drudgery." If our attitude is right, then our service comes from a heart of true love. True love does not depend on the worthiness of the recipient, but on the character of the giver. True love always gives with no thought of receiving.

Jeremiah 31:16b tells us, ". . . for thy work shall be rewarded, saith the Lord." What more could we ask for, when God has promised to bless our efforts? God's blessings always outweigh our giving. We give and give, because we love the Lord.

A certain family had experienced many different activities, and summer time was a very busy season. The minister husband and daddy had been scheduled for a week of meetings since early spring. There was a church project that had to be given considerably more time than had been allotted. Mothers and youth girls had been busy helping with the painting, varnishing, staining trim, and hanging wallpaper.

The youth had agreed to help both young and older families with their gardens as that summer's youth project.

Then there were visitors traveling through the area, stopping in unexpectedly for a meal or an overnight stay. There were elderly couples who needed young, strong arms and hands to help with jobs such as washing windows. There was a young mother next door, who had three small children and a tiny baby, who needed a girl to help her with her work. There was summer Bible school and the need of teachers.

These and many others were the demands on the family, when a daughter made the remark, "I think we are born for charity work!"

"Yes!" answered the mother, "We are!"

This is how the title of this chapter came into being, and it has been thought-provoking ever since!

After all, we are not our own; we are here to serve our Lord and Savior by serving our fellowmen, those around us, those in need, and those passing by. We as parents are responsible to instill this basic attitude into our children. As they mature and leave home to face the world, they are either going to follow their own pursuits or realize that they, too, are born for charity work. Often a child is a reflection of his or her parents, and at an early age!

Someone has nobly said, "Don't ask life, 'What can I get,' but 'What can I contribute?' "

If we live for the purpose of making a contribution

instead of asking what we can get, our lives will demonstrate that we are born for charity work. Not only will this be true for parents, but it will be carried on in the next generation, and generations to come.

> "If you have a work to do—do it now!
>   If you have a witness to give—give it now!
> If you have a soul to win—win him now!
>   If you have an obligation to discharge—
>   discharge it now!
> If you have a debt to pay—pay it now!
>   If you have a confession to make—make it
>   now!
> If you have a preparation to make—make it now!
>   If you have children to train—train them
>   now!
> Remember, time is passing by,
>   and you are passing out of time."
>
> *(Selected)*

Perhaps these questions come to all of us: What can I do? What is there to do? What does God expect of me and of my family? Just why was I created?

The life of Queen Esther is a striking example. As we think of these questions we sometimes ask ourselves, "Who knoweth whether thou art come to the kingdom for such a time as this?" (Esther 4:14b). God had a divine purpose for Queen Esther at that time, and no one else could come close to fulfilling that calling. Just so today, we are all called to "such a time as this," and God has a specific work for each of us. No one else is called of God to do our work. Therefore we must be vigilant, diligent, earnest, strong, and willing to carry out God's plan for us.

We are not all called to serve on the foreign field, yet we are called to support and encourage, to give of our time and talents. As we involve ourselves in bringing encouragement to those "out front," we can also involve our children. Encourage them to send to children their age a little remembrance of their birthday, or a greeting card and a letter at Christmas. Many write to missionaries on special occasions, but what about the times when a name comes to your mind and you lazily push off the idea to write a letter? More important yet, whisper a prayer for them when you think of them. Perhaps the missionary is especially in need of a prayer at that moment.

For years our family has been blessed by making Christmas bundles—each of our children makes one for a child their age. We would plan to go shopping just for the Christmas bundle items. What a joy for the children to pick out a small toy that they would have enjoyed for themselves, to give to another child.

The summer of 1975 was a busy one. A baby girl was added to our family in mid-July, leaving only three weeks to get the bundles together. Health had not permitted the project earlier. The idea of taking a three-week-old baby to go shopping for Christmas bundle items was almost overwhelming to me, but as usual the children were eager to go. Hating to disappoint them, I decided to undertake this one Saturday afternoon. My husband was gone on church work and had taken our nine-year-old son along.

It was a very warm, humid day and our Datsun had no air conditioning, but it was the last Saturday before the Christmas bundle baling, so there was no option but to go. I knew it would be a special treat for our girls aged ten and five. I placed the three girls in the Datsun pickup, with the ten-year-old in charge of the baby, and away we went! In spite of the heat and my apprehensions everything went well for about an hour. All of a sudden the baby started to cry, and would not be comforted! To make a long, frustrating story short, we hurriedly completed our shopping and rushed home, with a very fussy baby, a tired, weary mother, but two patient and happy little girls.

As time went on, I forgot about my frustration. One day, to our surprise, the mail carrier brought a letter from a faraway family, telling of the joy of receiving one of our Christmas bundles! What a reward! What an encouragement to continue on! Needless to say, each year the "shopping spree" got better than the year before.

A couple in our church has taken the responsibility to plan a desk calendar for a sister on the mission field. They buy a filler for the calendar and distribute the sheets to the church people. Parents, children, and all are asked to add a Scripture verse or quote, and sign their names. It may seem small, and yet it is a reminder for every day of the year that the church back home is thinking of her. My appreciation goes to the mother who first thought of this, and took time from her busy schedule to get the calendar together.

There are the teachers in our Christian day school, who give of their time, energy, and talents—and fix their lunches every day. Why not let your child bring home the teacher's lunch box and help you fix a lunch for the teacher? It doesn't have to be elaborate. Just knowing you take time to fix the lunch is rewarding enough! Take a minute longer and share your appreciation for the teacher by writing a note on her napkin.

Needless to say, it also adds a special touch to your children's day when you write a note on their napkin telling them that you love or appreciate them. Words of appreciation are welcome early in life.

The past school term, the first-grade teacher often had messages written on her napkin, which she would read to the children. To her surprise, one day a little girl brought her own napkin and said, "Read this to me!" Her mother had written a message on the child's napkin, and the little girl couldn't read it herself. As the teacher read the note, a smile appeared on the first-grader's face. After several days, nearly all of the class had notes in their lunches for the teacher to read to them. Imagine the joy of that teacher!

Perhaps it's a beginning of sprinkling encouragement and love into their lives, increasing as they grow older. As they are taught by example, it will become a part of their life and through their lives other people will be blessed. But most of all, God is glorified by the encouragement and love that is in their young hearts.

Lend a hand! "I am only one, but still I am one; I cannot do everything, but still I can do something; and because I cannot do everything, I will most gladly do the something that I can do." (Selected).

Imagine the difference it makes in our families, in the church, in the community, when we are all willing to lend a hand!

God's work will not suffer; one person or family or minister will not be overloaded because we are all aware that we are born for charity work and have "come to the kingdom" for such a time as this."

Giving Your Best

It's the hand we clasp with an honest grasp
    That gives a hearty thrill;
It's the good we pour into other's lives
    That comes back our own to fill.

It's the dregs we drain from another's cup
    That make our own seem sweet;
And the hours we give to another's need
    That make our life complete.

It's the burdens we help another bear
    That make our own seem sweet;
And the hours we give to another's need
    That make our life complete.

It's the burdens we help another bear
    That make our own seem light;
It's the danger seen for another's feet
    That shows us the path to right.

It's the good we do each passing day,
    With a heart sincere and true;
In giving the world your very best,
    Its best will return to you.

—Author Unknown

A Woman Given To Hospitality

by Anna Mary (Mrs. Bennie) Byler

When I was a child and lived on a farm, my mother would frequently receive a letter from relatives in Pennsylvania, informing her that they would soon be on their way to visit us.

"We've got to get the house in order; Grandma is coming," Mother would say.

We aired the straw-ticks, the guest bedroom; we swept the yard clean under the big weeping willow tree; we washed windows until they gleamed; we hauled out the carpets and beat them vigorously on the clothes line; we polished every piece of furniture and freshened the hall-ways with the dust mop.

At last everything was in order and Mom would be a bit more relaxed, knowing the house was in tip-top shape, ready for the visitors. Down through the years this seemingly has been our concept of hospitality—clean your house when expecting visitors, "cook up a storm" to impress them, put on clean clothes and wear a bright sunny smile.

We have just taken a glimpse at what hospitality was years ago, now let's briefly look at what the Bible says.

II Kings 4:8-17 gives one of the best examples of what

the Bible calls true hospitality. The Shunammite woman saw the need in a passerby—"a holy man of God" (v. 9). She was the one who visualized what would be ideal for Elisha. She was the one who brought the plan to her husband's attention, and together they worked to bring this to pass. "Let us make a little chamber, I pray thee, on the wall; and let us set for him there a bed, and a table, and a stool, and a candlestick: and it shall be when he cometh to us, that he shall turn in thither" (v. 10).

This possibly is a gift God has entrusted to us as sisters, but nevertheless, we must stay in our God-given place. Therefore, we as families can be more sensitive to the command of being hospitable.

As a woman given to hospitality, we must have a desire to make our visitors comfortable and supply their needs. It does not need to be elaborate, but homey; not many fineries, but the basic items! It should be a relaxing and restful atmosphere.

Do we think that providing all this, together with an elaborate, fancy, well-balanced meal for visitors, is real hospitality?

What about our families? How do they rate? Can we be one person to visitors and strangers, and quite someone else on the everyday level at home? The relaxed, homey atmosphere needed for visitors, should be the general atmosphere of our home for our husband and children on an everyday basis.

Webster defines hospitality as being generous, pleasant, inviting, beneficial to life, readily receptive, open.

Paul prayed for special blessings on the house of Onesiphorus, "for he oft refreshed me" (2 Tim. 1:16). Hospitality should refresh!

When Jesus came to Bethany "Martha received him

into her house" (Luke 10:38-42). Jesus felt welcome there.

Acts 12:12 reveals that Peter knew where the Christians were gathered and were diligently praying for his safety—at the home of Mary, John Mark's mother.

To Paul and his fellow laborers, Lydia said, "If ye have judged me fatihful to the Lord, come to my house, and abide there" (Acts 16:15).

Both Acts 18:1-3 and I Corinthians 16:19 speak of Priscilla and Aquilla's hospitality. Because they and Paul were of the same trade, Paul stayed at their house. In 16:19, Paul conveys to the Corinthians the greetings of "Aquilla and Priscilla, with the church that is in their house."

None of these passages mentions fancy homes or luxurious meals, but these women gave of themselves! Could it be that down through the years our concept of hospitality has been warped? Is it not true that hospitality begins in the heart, involving our attitudes more than the outward performance?

Some time ago our sewing circle sisters were studying the subject of being hospitable. After our family left for their day's duties, I hurried around trying to quickly get to our sewing. Then there were interruptions. A neighbor stopped by; the phone rang several extra times. As the minutes ticked by I was becoming more frustrated, knowing I'd be late. Then one more phone call revealed a much-needed stop at the drug store for a prescription.

All of a sudden I was struck with the thought that I'm only trying to impress the sewing circle sisters by being there early, but really I'm missing out on the true meaning of hospitality. After spending a few minutes in meditation and putting God first, I no longer felt the need to be there first. After all it is God, the One for whom and by whom I live, who allows my plans to be changed. When I finally got to the sewing, I could smile from the heart, because I knew I had been distracted for a purpose.

In our discussion, I honestly shared my experience and how it is the attitude of our hearts, rather than serving visitors, that God actually calls hospitality. Our desire to impress people is a selfish desire. One sister shared how she also had struggled that very morning, and had been cross with her family in order to get there, too. My heart was blessed to know that our character is what God knows we are; our reputation is only what people think we are! Hospitality does begin in the heart.

Someone said, "Hospitality is part of being a good steward, of showing gratitude for home itself."

On Resurrection Sunday, Jesus walked with two disciples to Emmaus. "But their eyes were holden that they should not know him" (Lu. 24:16). They thought He was a stranger. Yet, when they reached Emmaus, they constrained Him, saying, "Abide with us: for it is toward evening, and the day is far spent" (v. 29). They may have feared for this stranger's life if he should travel on that night. What a reward for their heartfelt hospitality, when they discovered that it was Jesus Himself!

In the Biblical commands concerning hospitality, the emphasis is not on an elaborately planned meal, for expected company.

But it seems to be the atmosphere of the home and the attitudes of the occupants that stands out. In fact, "a lover of hospitality, [is] a lover of good men, sober, just, holy, temperate" (Titus 1:8). That suggests moderation.

As ministers' families, we would all agree that being hospitable is not something we can regard or disregard as our moods change. We should first realize that our husband and children are special, and for their sakes we desire to keep our homes clean and pleasant, a place where our families love to be. Then we can be ready for guests, regardless if we are prepared for them or not. A Christian home should always be a place of order, cleanliness, and peace.

As we remember that Jesus is the Head of our home and heart, our motto should be, "If it is good enough for our husband and children, then it should also be sufficient for visitors.

If our hearts are hospitable, then our homes will also be such that unexpected visitors, known or unknown to us, can feel the Christ-like love and concern that prevail.

Early in married life our homes should be orderly. As children become a part of the family, they should be able to sense they are valuable and precious to the Lord and to us as parents, even though the house is less orderly. As they grow up in this environment they, too, will have a love and respect for visitors and, at a young age, feel the responsibility to help with the extra work of entertaining strangers and friends alike.

The minister's family, and especially the bishop's family, is often the first home contacted when someone wishes to visit the church or community. Therefore, it is very important that the minister's wife is given to hospitality (I Timothy 3:2; Titus 1:7, 8).

During our courtship years, my husband made a statement that I don't think I'll forget. The idea was that to him it was important to have the house in proper order and also food handy enough to make a quick, nourishing meal and not in a frenzied way. In our twenty-four years of marriage I have many times thanked God for canned meat, individually frozen steaks, canned vegetables and fruit, and a good supply of breakfast items, so I did not need to rush off to the grocery store at the first sign of visitors.

The attitude of the wife is so important. She should be just as concerned about cooking attractive meals for her family as for visitors. Thus, she is demonstrating to her family her love for the Lord.

If Jesus really is the Head of our home, it will be a home of order and contentment, and in turn it will be a witness for those we meet.

As our children grow up, we also need to encourage them to be hospitable by inviting their friends home for a meal or snack, and sharing a genuine interest in them. We as parents need to help plan a simple yet good meal, remembering to stay within our means.

One time my husband brought home a car load of visitors he had passed while driving the interstate. As they came off at the same exit, he invited them home just several minutes before dinner. Imagine my surprise when he arrived home with a car load of hungry people, but praise the Lord for a family who worked together, and the blessing of having planned ahead. The gas grill was ignited and individually wrapped hamburger steaks were prepared; while another person opened a jar of green beans, cooked some noodles, cut up some vegetables for salad, another person brought cookies from the freezer, and opened a jar of fruit.

As we visited we were all blessed to know that as we serve our fellowman, we are, indeed, doing it "as unto the Lord." Later, after the visitors were on their way, one of the children said, "That was fun!" And it was! It not only added a dimension in friendship, but it also brought a closeness to us as a family.

My husband leaves quite frequently for church work and revival meetings. He has often been blessed by small, kind deeds: a fresh bed; clean, crisp, air-scented sheets are so refreshing to a weary body; a cool, well-ventilated room where the windows can be opened or closed; shades or curtains that can easily be adjusted. At times fresh fruit was placed on his desk if a late supper was planned. Since he did not eat breakfast, a cup of hot tea or coffee was refreshing and very welcome.

If a desk is not a normal piece of furniture in the room, a card table and folding chair is adequate.

If possible a drawer can be emptied and offered to the evangelist to use for his personal belongings, both in the bedroom and also in the bathroom.

The offer to do his laundry has also been appreciated, especially if he was away from home for any length of time.

Some years ago there was a young man who "bached" for several months prior to his marriage. Often he would stop in as we were eating lunch or supper. We simply brought another chair, added an extra plate and he would join us. The fellowship meant much. Yet, it is important to keep in mind that men, and especially growing boys, appreciate a full course meal. To mothers it is reward enough to plan and fix a meal, and then to see everyone happily eating as well as fellowshipping.

Reflecting back to the story of Mary and Martha and their open door, Jesus must have loved to be there! So yet today, I believe we as wives still desire to keep our lives and homes in order so Jesus would feel welcome. Our families and strangers need to be received the same way.

Someone observed that being both a Mary and a Martha constitutes a total Christian woman who is "given to hospitality."

Martha, in the kitchen, serving with her hands
Occupied for Jesus, with her pots and pans.
Loving Him, yet fevered, burdened to the brim,
Careful, troubled Martha, occupied FOR Him.
Mary on the footstool, eyes upon her Lord,
Occupied *with* Jesus, drinking in His Word.
This one thing is needful, all else strangely dim.
Loving, resting Mary, occupied WITH Him.
So may we, like Mary, choose the better part
Resting in His presence, hands and feet and heart,
Drinking in His wisdom, strengthened by His Grace,
Waiting for His summons, eyes upon His face.
When He comes we're ready, spirit, will and nerve,
Mary's heart to worship, Martha's hand to serve.
This the rightful order, as our lamps we trim,
Occupied WITH Jesus, then *Occupied For Him.*

—*anonymous*

Kind words are the music of the world.

If I Had Known

If I had known in the morning
How wearily all the day
The words unkind
Would trouble my mind
I said when you went away,
I had been more careful, darling,
Nor given you needless pain,
But we vex our own
With look and tone
We might never take back again.
We have careful thoughts for the stranger,
And smiles for our sometime guest.
But oft for 'our own'
The bitter tone,
Though we love 'our own' the best."

There is something so tender and so healing; something so precious, when great, strong men are unfailingly kind, that a woman's heart grows strong, even under a heavy burden, when she is fed by kindness.

Communication –
Where Two Minds Meet

by Anna Mary (Mrs. Bennie) Byler

Have you ever driven along a country road and noticed a house that was once beautiful and new, but now with age and neglect it is a heap of ruin, in shambles? The windows are broken, the paint is peeling, the grass is long and unmowed. Bushes and shrubs are overgrown and unkempt; tin cans and rubbish add to the desolation.

This perhaps can be compared to communication between husband and wife—or rather, the lack of communication. It is a sad picture of the hurting couple.

"But speaking the truth [be sincere] in love, may grow up into him in all things, which is the head, even Christ" (Ephesians 4:15). It is God's plan for husband and wife, that we may continue to speak the truth in love and thereby continually grow up in Christ.

A dating couple usually does not lack for things to talk about, and they say they are so deeply in love that time just doesn't allow for all that needs to be communicated. But it does not have to all be said before marriage. Couples should continue to be open and feel the need of sharing long after the wedding bells have stopped ringing. So often the lack of communication is evident. "Can two walk together, except they be agreed?" (Amos 3:3).

Husbands and wives are basically different. That is why the home is God's classroom for molding and shaping us into mature people.

Peter Marshall spoke of communication as the fusion of two hearts, the union of two lives, the coming together of two tributaries, which after being joined together, all flow in the same channel, in the same direction, carrying the same burden of responsibility and obligation. That describes the meeting of two minds.

When there is open and true communication, there is always one transmitter and one receiver; one who speaks, and one who listens. Communication is also defined as speaking clearly, openly, honestly, getting on common union.

What we are at home is really who we are. That is who God knows we are. Since only seven percent of our communication is verbal, ninety-three percent is portrayed in the tone of voice, the expressions, and the attitudes. The home is the acid test. We can fool other people by being "Sunday Christians," but at home we are the person we really are in private where no one but God can see.

In many cases talking is a real struggle. Rather then using conversation to communicate, it is used to embarrass, to ridicule, or to joke. But it shouldn't hurt for husband and wife to talk. It won't if we use some basic ideas that lead to communication.

I Corinthians 13 has the answer. We must talk with love and truth in our voice. We must be longsuffering and kind (v. 4). Verse six tells us to speak truthfully; verse seven —we need to speak with understanding and trust toward our companion. With trust comes an optimistic outlook. We will persevere and not give up easily or label our situation as impossible.

Instead, so often we are negative, and become envious, selfish, and proud (v. 4). Our actions and words are rude, self-centered; we become touchy and easily provoked, and of course this leads to imagination and evil surmising. Then we become critical and find fault. This doesn't lead to openness or speaking clearly; neither do we reach a common union. Rather a lack of communication is the result. Satan is the author of anything less than God's best. He was able to bring dissension in the garden of Eden, and ever since that he is warring against God.

The story of Adam and Eve in Genesis three tells us the serpent came to Eve. Could this be where the lack of communication began? When husband and wife don't speak so they are understood, often the result is misunderstanding or lack of communication. Perhaps if Eve had consulted Adam, and together they would have approached the serpent, Eve might not have been deceived. We do notice communication was in the original plan of God. When Adam and Eve were in perfect harmony, "the Lord God visited them in the cool of the day" (Genesis 3:8).

Our personal devotion and dedication to God is of utmost importance, to be able to communicate as husband and wife. Ephesians 5:19-25 could be relating to our private communion with God. Sing, make melody, and give thanks to God always. Then submitting one to another as husband and wife; husbands love and wives submit.

"My voice shalt thou hear in the morning, O Lord; in the morning will I direct my prayer unto thee, and will look up" (Psalm 5:3)! If our private communication with God is vibrant, then as husband and wife we will also be convinced of the need together to meet with God in family devotions. When family devotions is part of a home, the atmosphere will be one of quietness and serenity.

God blesses with a good, open communication between parents and children in our home as we seek to instill a Godly respect in our families.

Since thirty-eight percent of communication is in the tone of voice and in our attitudes to life in general, it is so important that we are pleasant and cheerful. We must exercise patience even though we may need to remind family members numerous times of things that need their attention.

Some of us may be critical of Nicodemus for coming to Jesus by night, but recently I wondered if perhaps he was like we wives are in our homes. Our husbands are so busy, either with the concerns of the church and other people or with the task of making a living, that the only time left to discuss our dreams, concerns, cares, and differences is at night, after others are asleep.

This past fall, when our daughter started teaching school, was the first that Bennie and I were able to eat lunch together alone on a regular basis. Many have been the subjects that we have discussed, because earlier, if we didn't talk at night, many issues were left unspoken. Some developed into hard and deep rifts that we had to work and talk through. At times I struggled with the idea that the only time left for us to be together is when we sleep. However, God kindly reminded me that my husband belongs to Him; and I desire to please God and to do His bidding. Then again, I find peace and joy in our busy life. Often I need to go to the Bible for my encouragement, like David did in I Samuel 30:6, ". . . but David encouraged himself in the Lord."

Communication is not some exhilarating experience, but rather a deep love that has been tried by the "fire of adversity." This love grows in our lives as we confess when we are wrong saying, "I'm sorry," "Forgive me," or "I was wrong." Then we become teachable and easy to live with, and communication becomes a joy.

Upon everything that God places His blessing, Satan is right there to undermine it. SELF is the number one enemy to good communication. Because of self we find it hard or even impossible to accept God's dealing in our life. Lack of communicaton is not keeping the lines clear. There is no GUESS WORK in the happy marriage!

The following attitudes are enemies to good communication:

BITTERNESS—We must recognize "My times are in thy hand . . ." (Psalm 31:15). God always has the right to everything I would desire to have and cling to.

DEPRESSION—"In everything give thanks . . ." (I Thess. 5:18). "Rejoice in the Lord alway . . ." (Phil. 4:4). It is impossible to be depressed when we LOOK UP and see God in every circumstance.

RESENTMENT—It takes more energy to resent than it does to submit. "The foolishness of man preventeth his way, and his heart fretteth against the Lord" (Prov. 19:3).

COVETOUSNESS—"But godliness with contentment is great gain" (I Tim. 6:6). Nagging verbalizes a discontented spirit. So in order to be free from nagging, we must have and exercise a contented spirit. Count our blessings—what we have rather than what we don't have.

Husband and wife are not required to think alike, but to think together. If Christ is the goal of our lives then it will not be hard to be open and communicate freely.

We spouses dare not use sex to reward or to bargain

with our partners. According to one observation, the 60's were characterized in society by the attitude that "sex holds the couple together." Their love was gauged by their bedroom experience. Now, twenty-five to thirty years later, one look at the world tells us that their theory was not true. If it were true, our world would not be the wicked, violent place it is.

Sex is a gift of God, designed by God to be a blessing to both husband and wife. It is not controlled by saying the right words or acting a certain way. "Meaningful sex relationship comes when both husband and wife are appreciated, affirmed, loved, and secure in their love. Sex is not a repair kit; sex does not fix marriage any more than a new baby stabilizes a marriage! What marriage really needs is creative intimacy, and this may simply be sitting side by side, reading a book together, or holding hands. At times it may mean crying together and talking it out" (quote from Dean Martin).

Good marriages don't just happen; you make them happen. If we are concerned about our communication and desire to grow in our love relationship as husband and wife, then we will be willing to be open and teachable and together learn how to speak the truth in love.

Overcoming Communication Breakdown

1. Be open and honest. Don't live behind a mask; God knows.
2. Be teachable; let God direct you and allow each to help the other.
3. Talk from your heart. It should not hurt to talk. Submit one to another.
4. Pray together and ask God's blessing and wisdom. Reach decisions together.

5. If there is conflict or misunderstanding, don't part until you both had a good understanding.
6. Don't exaggerate using "always" and "never."
7. Think before you speak. Don't speak "off the top of your head." We should continually ask God to "keep the door of my lips" (Psalm 141:3). "He that answereth a matter before he heareth it, it is folly and shame unto him" (Prov. 18:13).
8. Listen when your partner speaks. Listen until he has completed his sentence. Listen with your heart!

Let us be quick to share appreciation love, care, concern, and kindness to those dearest to us, that we may be counted worthy to truly communicate in a Godly manner.

Submitting one to another

As "iron sharpeneth iron" (Prov. 27:17) so we must polish and sharpen each other's character if we want to be a help to each other in drawing closer toward God and maturity.

"But speaking the truth in love, may grow up into him in all things, which is the head, even Christ" (Eph. 4:15).

Lord, help me walk so close to Thee
     That those who know me best,
Can see I live as godly as I pray,
     And Christ is real from day to day.
I see some once a day, a year,
     To those I blameless may appear.
'Tis easy to be kind and sweet
     To people who we seldom meet.
But, in my home are those who see
     Too many times the worst of me.
My hymns of praise were best unsung,
     If He does not control my tongue.
When I am vexed and sorely tried
     And my impatience cannot hide,
May no one stumble over me
     Because Thy love they fail to see.
But, give me Lord, thru calm and strife
     A gracious and unselfish life;
And help me with those who know me best
     For Jesus' sake to stand the test.

—anonymous

Accepting The Call
Of An Evangelist

by Anna Mary (Mrs. Bennie) Byler

Can you say with heartfelt assurance, "Yes, Christ is Lord of all?"

For years I reasoned and bargained with God. "No, I don't want to be a deacon's wife. A deacon has too many unpleasant tasks to perform. I really don't want to be a minister's wife—he is asked to preach, spend lots of time studying and go for revival meetings. And I would be scared to stay at home alone with our children. I don't want to be a bishop's wife because of all the weighty matters of administration of church life. No, I don't want to!"

I rebelled, I resented, I bargained with God, yet God did not let me go my willful way. A minister ordination was held, and Bennie shared in the lot, yet was not chosen. A year later, he again was in the lot; again, he was not chosen. During the next two years, God brought me through some real trials. At the end of those two years, there was a deacon ordination, and Bennie was chosen.

In Ezekiel's time, God sought for a man (family) among them that should make up a hedge and stand in the gap before him in the land, that He should not destroy it. But God found none (22:30). God is still seeking for those families who should make up a hedge and stand in the gap. Is it possible that God cannot find any today?

We as wives can make it hard or even impossible for our husbands to really dedicate themselves wholly to the Lord's work, especially that of being an evangelist.

If we find it hard to have our plans changed, we are a hindrance to their work. What if we as a family have an annual vacation planned, and this year my husband is scheduled for a week of meetings instead? Can I gladly and willingly give up my plans for the Lord's sake? My attitude will also be reflected in the children's attitudes and in their support.

Also, I as his wife can be overly concerned about my personal needs, rather than being willing to let my husband go. Instead, I want that new living room suite or a larger house—it could be anything. But I want to be willing, especially when I think of all God's rich blessings! How can I say "No?"

A new church house was under construction for our congregation. The basement was finished and used for worship services on Sunday. Then on Monday morning the place was reorganized to be a classroom for the next five days. Bennie was busy as chairman of the building committee and also of the school board. He spent lots of time at the school, and again getting the sanctuary ready for services.

Because Bennie was employed by another construction crew, he would work eight hours and from there go to the church construction site and work until late at night. At times the children and I would take his supper to the job and he would eat before going to this second job. Quite frequently, he would take his young son along.

I spent many hours at home alone with the children, and at times I felt very resentful. If I allowed God to have His way and to give me joy in the midst of my trials, we would experience and enjoy many rich hours together reading Bible stories, working on the lawn or in the garden together. (Most of the work at home was left to me.)

Over and over I needed to renew my commitment to God and give myself, my family, and all to His service. If I resented my lot in life, God seemingly kept His finger on that very spot in my life until I was willing to yield. Over and over I was tried, and little by little, I yielded.

Yes, now I was willing to become a deacon's wife. Yet, I had one reservation! That was, my husband couldn't go away as an evangelist. I had now committed myself to be a faithful deacon's wife and also be willing to help in those unpleasant tasks I had pictured as the work of a deacon.

The first Sunday we had services in the new church building, the church voted to have a deacon ordination on Marcy 19, 1972—our eighth wedding anniversary!—and Bennie was ordained.

During the weeks that followed, I felt very frustrated and as I was looking through our meager library, I found a book on prayer. As I read chapter after chapter, I dedicated myself to God with the stipulation that deacons are not evangelists nor become bishops. God did not let me take my own way but continued to work in my life. As I yielded, I found more peace and joy and more blessings. Of course, my desire grew to be all God wanted our family to be, and to let go of my husband's life.

Eighteen months later, God called Bennie to the office of bishop. Our children enjoy listening to the cassette tape of the ordination, when the bishop prayed for the children, mentioning them by name.

As the ordination was approaching, I was searching for some encouragement in the Bible. One Saturday morning as I opened my Bible, Ezekiel 33:7 stood in bold letters—"So thou, O son of man, I have set thee a watchman unto the house of Israel . . ." When I read the verse, I did not feel resentful but said, "Yes, Lord! Not my will but Thine be done." But deep down in the smallest crevices of my heart I said, "But no evangelist." When the charge was given, I listened carefully if his charge included ". . . and do thou the work of an evangelist." I didn't hear the phrase, so as before I felt a bit relieved.

Several years went by and one evening a call did come to inquire if Bennie would consider a week of revival meetings at Calvary Bible School. Some months later another call came and so, little by little I resigned. How could I say "No!" when there were so many who needed to hear the gospel. So God has been working in my life, and I am still saying "Yes" to God and "No" to self.

In the book of Judges, the life of Deborah is a good example of a woman of courage. Her story helps us understand that in every age God will dwell with those who sincerely seek Him. Deborah was filled with God's wisdom. She did not seek popularity among her own people by leaving her home to have a public office. Yet because of her spiritual character people sought her out to find help for their problems. God also trusted her with a message for Barak, because God knew that Deborah would wisely help Barak do the task instead of doing it for him. (Barak should have trusted God but instead he was fearful.) Even though Deborah went along to battle, she stayed in the background and helped organize and develop his battle strategy. Even in the church today and especially as the wife of an evangelist, I need to encourage my husband to be strong and to preach the Word without fear or favor of man, but rather fearing God and preaching the truth in love.

"For we are laborers together with God . . ." (I Cor. 3:9a). Could there be a greater blessing than to know that we are laborers together? Many are the ways I can encourage and pray for his message especially while he is preparing the message and as he is holding meetings. This is one way we can labor together.

As wives we face the question, should I go along or should I stay home with the children? Often as I am faced with the question, Bennie and I discuss the matter and we both feel more comfortable when I stay home. Our children would nearly always go with us to the Ministers' Fellowship Meetings or if he would go for Sunday meetings. But as they reached school age, I stayed home more. What a blessing to be there to answer their questions and to care for problems as they arose. Good communication begins when the children are babies and continues on, even when they are grown.

Later, God did bless so we can have a business at home. He has also blessed us with faithful church brethren who kept the business going when Bennie was called away to preach. Our son, after completing school, also faithfully took care of the business many times when Bennie was called to preach.

There are various ways that we as wives can help our children support their daddy when he is called to be an evangelist. Slipping notes or a special card into your husband's suitcase can be a real encouragement. Also children sharing notes is very impressive and draws the family together. One time I dropped a Hershey chocolate kiss in each pair of my husband's socks to remind him of my love for him. It can be special to have a short prayer meeting about the time Daddy is to begin his message.

Visitors stopping in are an added blessing. The children and I have hosted a number of visitors who came to visit while Bennie was gone. He also has been challenged by some who say they come to see if we lived what he preached. This too has broadened our family's horizons.

John 6:43 reminds us, "Murmur not among yourselves." Murmuring hinders God's blessings. If we are serious about Christ being Lord of all, we will have no time or energy to murmur and complain.

I still need to remind myself that "we are not our own, we are bought with a price: therefore, glorify God in your body, and in your spirit, which are God's" (I Cor. 6:19, 20).

Last, but not least, it is very important that we as wives provide a neat, homey, orderly "little Eden oasis" within our four walls, where all is quiet and serene. Home is the place where we as a family can close the door to the outside world and can enjoy God's Garden of Eden here on earth, where God can come and visit the evangelist's family "in the cool of the day" (Genesis 3:8a).

Leave your prayers to God
who knows when to give
how to give
what to give.

Pressed out of measure, and pressed to all length,
Pressed so intensely, it seems, beyond strength;
Pressed in the body and pressed in the soul;
Pressed in the mind till the dark surges roll.
Pressed by foes and the pressure from friends
Pressure on pressure till life nearly ends.

Pressed into knowing no help but God,
Pressed into loving the staff and the rod;
Pressed into liberty where nothing clings,
Pressed into faith for impossible things,
Pressed into living a life in the Lord,
Pressed into giving a Christ-life outpoured.

—*Author Unknown*

Saying "No" Graciously

by Anna Mary (Mrs. Bennie) Byler

"Mononucleosis . . . rest" were words we heard one busy spring day. What a contrast from what we had planned!

Traveling, attending an ordination, visitors, day jobs, summer Bible School, youth meetings: all these and more were on the agenda, but instead of our plans, God chose to stop us in our tracks! Now! Where do we go from here? We are brought to a crossroad of decision: either we fret and complain, or we see God also in the "stops" as well as the steps.

"The steps of a good man are ordered by the Lord" (Ps. 37:33). So also are the "stops." Note the difference one vowel makes!

The question comes to all of us . . . . Are we willing to accept the "stops" as well as the steps of the Lord? Can we find contentment in staying at home when we would rather be going? How willing are we as wives and mothers to change our wants and plans for the stops of the Lord? Perhaps this is one area where more is "caught" than taught! Our contentment or discontentment rubs off on our children.

Could this be the reason there is so much restlessness among our youth today?

When they were children growing up, we parents were not content at home, and we needed to be on the move evening after evening. Now we are waking up to see our children and youth even more involved than we had been, with no consciousness of time when they are gone.

There are some parents and some churches that have seen the need of a curfew for their youth. Yet if we, as parents, do not abide within that range, perhaps it's our problem rather than that of the youth.

The question that faces all of us is, "How can I be all I should be for God?" The answer isn't found in going, but in being quiet before God!

Someone has said, "It's not the Doings and Goings that are lacking, but the Being!"

Nehemiah 8:10b, "The joy of the Lord is your strength." This is a common phrase used among us, and how thankful we are to know that God's strength knows no limits. Yet we, as frail dust, must recognize we do have our limits. So somewhere there is a point where God wants us to say "No" graciously.

Perhaps next to being quiet before God is the ability to know our limits and be willing to let someone else do what we cannot do.

How often we are confronted with the questions, "Shall my husband go?," "Shall my husband be involved in a given situation?," or "Shall we say 'No' graciously?"

The first question to consider is, "Is it God's will?" God does open and close doors. If it's an invitation to preach the Word, it may mean a sacrifice for the pastor's wife.

Let us consider for a brief moment how the call to go and preach may affect us as wives.

If our relationship with God is a precious experience, we will be willing to allow our husbands to go and preach, even though it may mean the living room will not be remodeled right away. Or the vacation we as a family had planned may need to be postponed, or even cancelled. If we really trust God's best, we'll be willing to say "Yes" to God and "No" to our own desires.

Then, too, when husband and wife have a good relationship, they will be able to discuss and come to a mutual understanding of what God would have for their family at this time.

Another aspect to consider is the children. The wife and mother's attitude will largely be the deciding factor, whether or not their Daddy should be gone again, whether or not they will consider it their responsibility to pray and encourage him in his work.

Does the father have a good relationship with his children? It is very important, if we want God's blessing on the ministry God has entrusted to us.

Years ago there was a bishop who was called on quite frequently to help solve church problems. Finally, after a number of such requests and times of absences (when the son always needed to carry the extra responsibility at home), he soberly told his dad, "I wish the churches would behave so you could stay at home more."

Some time ago our teen-aged daughter was talking to her father. After several attempts she finally said, "Daddy, please lay the newspaper down and look me straight in the eyes." She needed her daddy's full attention! So often we give our children only grunts and nods—answers in a half-hearted way—or our "leftover" time. This is not good enough!

There are times when the atmosphere of the home isn't what God desires. Therefore it is important for us as parents to be sensitive to the *needs* of our children. Being sensitive if all is not well, by God's grace we can make amends by listening more intently. If all is not well at home, wise is the father who heeds the warning signs and says "No" graciously to invitations to be away from home for a lengthy period of time.

We, as parents, need to wake up and take notice of our children. We seemingly have time for all the phone calls, the business, other people's problems, the cares of this world, and yet have too little time for our families at home. It's at home, where too often we let angry words fly and are impatient when not everyone steps to "my tune," when perhaps it is our fault, as parents, because we are too involved to really take time to enjoy the little things of life.

We think we don't have time to stop and stroke the cat, who so happily rolls over to show her love. The roses and other flowers continue to share their beauty, and in our hurry we fail to stop and allow God to show us Himself in the fragrance of the perfection of the flowers.

The cool breeze floats through the open window, and we are too busy to enjoy the cooling effect of the refreshing air. The night sounds lull us to sleep night after night, and we are so engrossed in the pursuit of life that when we finally do get to bed, we barely remember falling in.!

Then as the years are speeding on, we wake up to the fact that our children are grown and have demands of their own. We wonder why they don't have time for us, to do those errands we no longer can do. While our children are in the molding age, we must take time for them, to be their best friend, to answer their questions honestly and meet their needs that only parents can meet.

May I say that there is where a large responsibility falls on us as mothers. The way we guide the house and family can help our children to have a feeling of belonging, when God has chosen to add many responsibilities to the husband and daddy.

Then, when we, as families, are united in our efforts, God can truly be the the Center of our lives, the Goal of our hearts. We then can reach out more effectively because we have learned by His grace to be who God wants us to be. And we are also able to delegate responsibility, because we have learned to say "no" graciously, and not feel guilty!

> There are hands that help and comfort,
>   Hands that plan and teach:
> Hands that reach and hands that strive
>   For the goal just out of reach;
> Hands that work and play;
> Friendly hands and loving hands
>   That soothe life's cares away.
> But praying hands are dearest
>   In the sight of God above;
> For in their sweet and earnest clasp
>   Is reverence and love.
> No hands can do an unkind act
>   Nor cause another care—
> Nor sin against our Father's love,
>   When they are clasped in prayer.

Come Ye Apart

"Come ye apart and rest awhile,"
        The Lord and Master said,
To His disciples for He knew
        That they too needed bread!

Come ye apart and rest awhile,
        Our Saviour knows the need,
Of quiet time—of time "well-spent,"
        Oh, may we thus take heed!

Come ye apart and rest awhile,
        And then take time to share
Some precious moments with the Lord
        And ask of Him His care!

And when vacation comes and goes,
        Our lives have been refreshed,
If Christ has been our constant Guide—
        Time will have been "well-spent!"

                by Martha (Mrs. David) King

Vacations: I Need The Quiet

by Amanda (Mrs. Roman) Mullet

Rest is as essential to life as work is. Even for work's sake, it is important. It renews the individual, restoring his God-given powers and enabling him to do his best.

Jesus, as our Example, knew how to rest as well as how to work. His work in the carpenter's shop was a preparation for the work of preaching. It acquainted Him with the joys and sorrows of the poor, to whom it was afterwards His privilege to perform His ministry. He was in this school of experience for approximately twenty-one years.

We presume that He was eager for the work which lay before Him. It appears that He waited hidden in the country till mind and body were mature and ready for that great work.

But in the midst of His work He also took means to maintain His liberty and peace of mind. When the multitude pressing in on Him grew too large and stayed too long, He withdrew Himself into the wilderness. Sometimes He would disappear, to refresh His body and His soul by casting it on the bosom of God.

When He saw how wearied and exhausted His disciples were, he would say, "Come ye yourselves apart into a desert place, and rest a while" (Mark 6:30-34). For even in

171

the most spiritual work it is possible to lose oneself.

Jesus said, "Foxes have holes, and the birds of the air have nests; but the Son of man hath not where to lay his head" (Luke 9:58). Could it be that He went to the mountain or to the desert to rest and pray because He had no home of His own? Was it because of being rejected? These are all things we are not completely sure of, but He is our perfect Example, and we long to be His followers as closely as we know and understand how.

How then shall we "come apart and rest a while?" We don't really use that term in our day, do we? We call it a "vacation." Webster's dictionary says vacation is a period of rest and freedom from work, study, and other activity. It does not really say how long, where or when. So possibly we would say one of the first and best places to be would be in our homes, a shelter from the pressures around us. Gather the family members around the fireside, where love and conviction rest, enjoying leisure, but not laziness, with a happy togetherness—and close the door to the outside world.

Try picnicking in the back yard; listening to the night sounds; watching the little ones catching fireflies; having a heart-to-heart talk with your teen-ager; just being there.

Vacations away from home can also be very beneficial. If we like geography, God's nature, meeting people, camp fires, and cook outs . . . and do not mind compact living, solid beds and unattractive bathroom facilities, we're out for a real retreat. This, however, takes preparation.

Sometimes the expression is made, "I just have to get away," or "we need to go on a vacation to have family togetherness." Some of us then would not have much family life if we would depend on vacations. A certain woman was asked what they did that their family is so close, and they are all members of the church? Her insightful reply was, "Many times we were all at home when most of you were going away."

Then who all goes on vacation? We would all agree "the whole family" . . . with a few exceptions. There are times when it is almost impossible for all to go; then, arrangements are made accordingly.

When shall we go on vacation? Looking back over the example of Jesus, we realize He did not have a wife and children; therefore, He made ways for His rest such as we possibly do not. Perhaps on the spot, without preliminary plans, He withdrew Himself. Sometimes He simply disappeared.

We, however, make plans. There are times when we get tired and weary, perhaps over-anxious to go on vacation away from home. Like Jesus, however, we should always remember to put first things first. Our loyalty to Jesus should be preeminent. No other person, no other pleasure, no other thing in the world should come before Him.

When He saw our lost condition, He put us first. He did not think of His own pleasure or comfort, but was thinking of us. This cost Him His life, but He was loyal to us. We then, should be loyal to Him, and use discretion when planning our vacation.

So wherever we do our vacationing (rest and freedom from work and study), let us think of Jesus with His kind and compassionate manner when He said to His disciples, "Come ye yourselves apart and rest a while."

Heaven's Very Special Child

A meeting was held quite far from earth
"It's time again for another birth,"
Said the Angels to the Lord above,
"This special child will need much love."

His progress may seem very slow,
Accomplishments he may not show
And he'll require extra care
From the folks he meets down there.

He may not run or laugh or play
His thoughts may seem quite far away
In many ways he won't adapt,
And he'll be known as handicapped.

So let's be careful where he's sent
We want his life to be content.
Please, Lord, find the parents who
Will do a special job for You.

They will not realize right away
The leading role they're asked to play
But with this child sent from above
Comes stronger faith and richer love.

And soon they'll know the privilege given
In caring for this gift from Heaven.
Their precious charge, so meek and mild
Is Heaven's very special child.

—*Author Unknown*

A Ministry To
Special Children

by Rachel (Mrs. Emanuel) Smucker

"We know that all things work together for good to them that love God, to them who are the called according to his purpose" (Romans 8:28). We didn't realize prior to our son's birth how much we would need this promise. What a privilege the child of God has to be assured that God makes no mistakes!

It's every couple's dream to have healthy children. This naturally was our desire, but God had some additional plans for us. I clearly remember the day I prayed for the baby in my womb. I asked God to bless us with a healthy child, never knowing that God had something else in mind.

Emanuel and I both loved children. We were blessed with a little boy and a little girl, and enjoyed working together on the farm. We were anticipating our third child. It was a beautiful autumn morning when the doctor announced, "You have given birth to a healthy, chubby baby boy." Our hearts could hardly contain the blessed joy a newborn child brings to a father and mother. This was our first time for natural childbirth, and it was a blessed experience.

John Mark weighed 8 pounds 4 ounces, and we

thought he was progressing normally. At five months we noticed that John wasn't holding his head like he should have been. We mentioned it to the doctor at his next checkup. The doctor sent him to the hospital where they did a series of tests. Their diagnosis was that John Mark is a slow child. What a relief it was to us! Our child appeared normal just like I had prayed for.

At nine months, there were more tests and more waiting. This time we weren't prepared for the shocking news. The doctors were suspicious of slight retardation. Again we were given hope that John Mark was normal when the doctor said that he questioned his big, bright, brown eyes.

Three months later John had another checkup. This time he was diagnosed as having cerebral palsy. We weren't familiar with the term, but we made a study of it. Cerebral palsy affects the motor coordination and usually happens during conception or childbirth. I still did not dream that our son would never walk or talk to me. I'd never hear him say, "Mommy, I love you."

Praise the Lord, He only takes us one day at a time, and He promises never to give us more than we are able to bear. "There hath no temptation taken you, but such as is common to man, but God is faithful, who will not suffer you to be tempted above that ye are able, but will with the temptation also make a way to escape, that ye may be able to bear it" (I Corinthians 10:13).

I remember so vividly how I felt two years later, putting John Mark into his special chair, and into a little yellow school bus. I walked back to the house in tears. I thought no one could care for my baby like I could, and John Mark was completely helpless. I whispered a prayer that God would be close to him.

School turned out to be a highlight for him. He learned to communicate with his eyes, looking up for "yes" and down for "no." His eyes are the only muscles he can control. We really count it a blessing, for this is how we communicate.

John was almost four years old when his brother J. Wendell was born. The doctor watched me closely throughout my pregnancy. It was another natural delivery. Every day I would hold our baby and check and double check his progress. I remember his hearty cry, and everything appeared normal. At three months of age we noticed some of the same symptoms that John had shown. A few weeks later, the doctor again announced, "Your son is also a cerebral palsy child." What a shock it was to us! I still remember the spot where Emanuel and I were, driving along, when he looked over at me and said, "Honey, either we can accept this, be happy, and make life nice for us and those around us; or else we can choose to reject it, be miserable, and make life hard for those we love." Emanuel was such a support to me; he would always have a Scripture verse that was so fitting and challenging.

We had gotten to be good friends with the social worker. One day when she stopped by, she bluntly stated, "You know, marriages either break or are made better because of these handicapped children." I often pondered that statement. I'm convinced you really learn to communicate at a time like this. Emanuel had a way of knowing that it was time for a "special date," when just the two of us did something together. At times it was just to go for a cup of coffee and to sit and talk. We soon learned of some faithful, reliable baby-sitters, and still today these baby-sitters are special friends of John Mark.

At four years of age, J. Wendell went home to be with

the Lord. He was greatly missed, especially by his brother. They would always be seen side by side on their mats on the floor or in their wheelchairs. We will always remember John's smile when we told him that J. Wendell went home to be with Jesus. He smiled and related to us that he's happy for J. Wendell. He could now walk and talk. Oh, the faith of a child! We have learned many lessons from John Mark, especially his patience and the way he accepts his handicap.

John was 20 years old on September 28, 1989, and he enjoys life. He knows God has a special purpose for him. He is our prayer warrior. The Lord knew we needed him. Many friends in the church tell him about different concerns, and he prays for them. He also gets to know many secrets, such as engagements, etc., for they know he won't tell anyone.

One of his highlights is going to the barn every morning and evening. Emanuel takes him along out early in the morning. John is our alarm clock. He's very concerned that his brothers get out in time, and that they do their chores right. He knows all the cows by their names and their pedigrees from a few generations back.

We would never have asked God for a handicapped child, but today we can't help but thank God for John Mark. Had we know all the blessings in store for us, many days would have been easier. That's where we need to trust the Lord, for He knows best.

Emanuel often reminds me that God has a plan, a blueprint for each one of His children. The closer we follow the blueprint, the better it will be for us. We thank God for the support of family, friends, and our other children. They have all been very supportive.

Don't shy away from the handicapped. They need you. Just relate to them like you would to any other person.

They too have needs and want to be understood.

One day our 7-year-old nephew told his mother that he hoped their next baby would be handicapped. His amazed mother wondered why. "So we can go to camps and retreats like Uncle Emanuels do," he answered. All those words of encouragement have meant so much to our family.

I thank God for my loving and supporting husband. He feeds John Mark, which is very difficult. A few years ago John completely bit off his lower lip. It was caused by clamping his mouth tightly shut over the years. Today he weighs 30 pounds, which was his weight since he was 5 years old.

I never once heard Emanuel complain about anything concerning John Mark. He and his daddy have a very close relationship.

We as a family feel these trials have been great stepping-stones and have drawn us closer to God and to each other. Trials are to make us better, and not bitter.

Questions:

1. What were some of your first feelings after discovering your child was handicapped?

You go through different stages; one of these stages was—"This just would not happen to us." Then the time comes when you have to face reality. The most important thing is to talk about it. Emanuel and I learned to communicate well, and we probably wouldn't have learned that otherwise.

2. What are some signs of denial at an early stage?

There are different reactions from different parents. One of these denial stages is going from doctor to doctor, looking for hope. This is something most parents go through. Advice and hints from other parents are helpful, but there are times when we need to work through our own situation.

3. How did you handle this with your other children?

The siblings will handle it much the same way as the parents cope with it. The sooner they learn that these children were put into our home for a special purpose, the better it will be. If the situation is handled as normally as possible, they will also benefit from the blessings.

4. Who were some helpful support groups to you as parents?

Parents' groups are terrific. It is good to talk with other mothers such as in the mothers' meetings at S. June Smith. There were times when I felt all I needed was a listening ear, and I soon learned where those people were.

5. What are some things to say to parents of handicapped children?

There are times when there are no right things to say. No matter what people say, it will be the wrong thing when we are hurting. Then there are times when we feel no one understands. I try not to let this distress me, for I know my husband, children, and some very dear friends care. I often think of what my friend Joyce told me one time. She said, "There are five people reaching out to help, and only one that gives a hurting remark." We need to focus on the handful of people that care, instead of the one person that doesn't. How precious it is that we have special friends in whom we can confide. They always understand and are such an encouragement.

6. What were your most difficult situations?

I'd say school placement was the most difficult. Now looking back, we marvel how the Lord worked it all out. You know, what seems to be our greatest concern usually turns out to be the best blessing.

7. Do you feel this experience has strengthened your marriage?

Yes, having a handicapped child definitely helped our marriage. I will never forget how one of the school counselors told me that many marriages ended in divorce because of a handicapped child. Any trial will either strengthen or break a marriage. That statement was a bit scary. During pressure, a marriage will not be at a standstill, but praise the Lord, He helped us have a better marriage.

Most important is the need to communicate, so Emanuel and I have learned to set aside a time for us to talk and relax, just the two of us. It's amazing how Emanuel is tuned in and knows that it's time for another date! It really is important for the husband to suggest a date; the wife will look forward to these times, and it actually helps her to keep her sanity at times. I'll let you in on a little secret. I really need these dates now that we have teenagers, almost more because of them than because of John Mark. Do you see all the benefits that are ours because of our handicapped children? I know I would take these teenage scenes a lot more seriously, had I not learned back there to work through some of these difficult situations. I will probably find an excuse for these dates when the children all leave the nest! These really are times we both enjoy, and they help us through the next stages again.

We need to be sensitive to one another's needs.

When I start feeling sorry for myself, Emanuel comes up with another of this lectures, how we need to work through this problem, since no one else is going to do it for us. I really don't know how I would have handled John Mark and J. Wendell without Emanuel. He helped me so much, and I need him in everything. He really is great.

Many times these handicapped children have served as our teachers, and we have learned through these experiences that there are blessings in the midst of trials. We are not our own, but we are here to bring glory to God.

❧

About the Writer

The Smucker family lives in Lancaster, Pennsylvania, and has been a real challenge to many people. They have a real ministry in relating to other parents of special children. They have a family of eight children and live on a farm. John Mark is a farmer at heart, and Emanuel usually takes him along to the barn, or for other activities. Their testimony as a family is that no matter what our situation, the Lord gives the needed grace, but it's up to us to accept His grace and learn from the experience that He allows in our lives.

❧

John Mark was granted his desire on January 3, 1991. He lived for the time he would be freed from his earthly limitation and be perfect in the presence of Jesus.

Even though he is greatly missed by his family, their testimony is:

<blockquote>
Mourning? — No!
Missing ? — Yes!
Rejoicing? — Forever!
</blockquote>

If we fear circumstances,
they control us
but
if we fear God,
He controls us.

Forgive Us

> . . . unless I can forgive this one
> who has hurt me so badly
> rejecting me so fully,
> I can expect nothing less
> than the pain of like rejection
> both now and in eternity, seeing how
> God in Christ so fully forgave me
> my every rebellion and wrong:
> Lord, God, I do want to forgive—
> remind me, hold me, help me!

As We Forgive Others.

—*Pollyanna Sedziol*

Coping With Accusations From Within The Church Family

"Give Me This Mountain" (Joshua 14:12)
by Amanda (Mrs. Roman) Mullet

C aleb is an amazing example for the people of God. Moses had sent Caleb from Kadesh-barnea to spy out the land. Caleb reported back to Moses what he felt was the truth. However, ten of the spies who had gone with them frightened the people and discouraged them from entering into the promised land.

Now since Caleb followed the Lord, Moses told him, "the section of Canaan you have desired shall belong to you and your descendants forever." Caleb continues to give his testimony of how young he was when he was first called to spy out the land. Then he goes on to say, "Today I am 85 years old, and I'm as strong as I was when Moses sent us out on that first journey, so, therefore give me this mountain, I shall be able—if so be that the Lord will be with me."

The experience of a minister's wife, and the story of Caleb are similar in that we also need to give heed to our calling and be obedient to God and His Word. It is of great importance to have our focus on the things of God, and on what He commands. If we become frightened and discouraged (difficulty-conscious) we tend to shrink from our

185

responsibilities, degrading ourselves, and hindering those who are in the church family.

What is our response, then, when accusations come which are true? Our first impulse may be to defend ourselves in the matter. But this would bring disrespect and disgrace to us and our ordained companion.

We need to be open (the church is as our mirror), acknowledge our wrong, confess it, and thank the individual for being kind and scriptural enough to bring the matter to our attention.

Whether or not the person confronting us has the right attitude is not the important question. What really matters is that we respond properly, in meekness and true humility. "For we are members one of another" (Eph. 4:25).

Then what of false accusations? These can be real shockers. Most of us have been assailed by false accusations, or ridiculed for just simply holding the church standard.

These rejections of God's Word and the work of His ordained ministers do not always disappear with time. Some make sport of what Christians stood for years ago (as it's reflected in the church standards) and tell them as "tales that are told," but let us remember that disobedience is still as the sin of witchcraft (I Sam. 15:23).

Your life and mine are telling the tale of our own spiritual temperature. These experiences may be stumbling blocks or steppingstones to us, depending on our response. I recall the time when I was tempted to question the wisdom of God for permitting me to be in this position. I looked back to my childhood days when I stood beside the bed of my dying mother, and she held my little hand in hers and would say, "I wish I could take you with me." Going through this difficulty and discouragement, I wondered, "Why, Lord, had her wish not been granted?" Then I think of David in distress, when he said, "Oh that I had wings like a dove! For then would I fly away, and be at rest" (Psalm 55:6).

What about Elijah with his flaming passions and powerful prayers? After all that God had done through him, we see him weak, downcast, embittered and unhappy, as if he had never known real victory. Loneliness had crept in on him. We, too, may be tempted at times to sit under our "juniper-bush" and to say, "It is enough."

We all have our dejections, defeats and despairs. They are partly from the nature of our work as a "help meet" to our dear companion's calling. It was God who brought Elijah back to his former good and sweet spirit. Faithful obedience and loving service renewed his zeal. His faith, his fearlessness, his scorn of evil, his prayerfulness, his devotion to Israel and to God, were all restored because of his total commitment and obedience to God.

What then, is our response? God does not ask anything of us that He does not enable us to fulfill. "Now therefore give me this mountain . . . if so be the Lord will be with me . . . then I shall be able." We need to forgive, we need to stay strong, regardless of the mountain God places before us. No matter how young we are (like the lad David meeting Goliath) or how old (like Caleb at 85), where God's finger points, there His hand will make a way.

"For this is thankworthy, if a man for conscience toward God endure grief, suffering wrongfully" (I Peter 2:19). "By this shall all men know that ye are my disciples, if ye have love one to another" (John 13:35).

Does God expect more from a minister's family? Paul gives instructions for the qualifications of bishops, deacons, and their wives (I Tim. 3:1-13; Titus 1:5-9), and I would presume that the evangelist and co-minister would be in the same category. And since this is God's Word, we assume that the congregation has a right to expect more from the minister's family. "God giveth more grace as the burdens increase." The minister is to rule well his own house, and to have his children in subjection with all gravity.

Just because my husband is a minister, does not automatically make me a woman of great wisdom and understanding. Does it not humble us however, that we in our unworthiness were chosen to be workers in this area? We therefore need to be prayer warriors, commit ourselves to the task and be a support to our husbands, and to the work of the church.

Accusations, true or false, can make us grow, bringing many blessings with them. Young (chosen) sisters, take courage. It is never easy to understand why troubles and sorrows come, but it is certain that we will never experience spiritual growth without them . . . "So give me this mountain."

It is not success
that God rewards,
but always the faithfulness of doing His will.

Blessed Is The Woman

who has
a sparkle in her eyes,
a song on her lips,
a spring in her step,
a warmth in her touch,
a depth to her beauty,
a purpose to her life,
a joy in her faith,
a hope in her breast, and
a love in her heart.

—Submitted by Barbara Hershberger

Starting In As Number Two

(Not Having Been A Number One)
by Eunice (Mrs. Wilford) Stutzman

"The will of God will not lead where the grace of God cannot keep." Does that include stepping into a ready-made family? Yes! Stepping into a ready-made family is a tremendous undertaking. It is a wonderful, yet humbling experience. It is special to be chosen to fill such a place, yet overwhelming. It makes you echo Ruth: "Why have I found grace in thine eyes, that thou shouldest take knowledge of me?" (Ruth 2:10).

God's will must be sought without any selfish reservations. Consider these areas carefully and prayerfully. Am I willing to give up some of my interests for the sake of filling needs in another's life? Can I fill the role of a mother, not having given birth to a child myself; let alone becoming a grandmother and mother-in-law all in one order? Am I capable of meeting the emotional, spiritual, and physical needs that exist in the family? Will the sudden responsibilities of being a minister's wife overwhelm me, not having been with him in his ordination, and growing into the role? Can I accept another's children as my own? Will they accept me as a mother? And the list of questions does not end there.

For me, the responsibility loomed as an enormous mountain: a mountain too high to scale, the circumference too great to get around it, and no way to tunnel through it. When I shared my fears with my future husband his answer was, "We don't approach it as a mountain. We just take one day at a time."

Searching for the Lord's will, being assured of His direction, realizing that of myself I could not, being confident that the Lord would undertake, I was willing to say again with Ruth: ". . . for whither thou goest, I will go; and where thou lodgest, I will lodge: thy people [congregation] shall be my people, and thy God my God." And I add, "Thy children my children."

Sharing the grief of a spouse is very essential in beginning your life as Number Two. Being joined as one flesh, grief is sensed more easily and weeping or grieving with a companion comes naturally. With a compassionate ear we listen to recollections of his former companion, considering his loss our own. We become aware of the adjustment it is for him to have given up the one he dearly loved and then to transfer that love to another. This awareness is a challenge to be the utmost for his good, making it easer for him to love.

Since time is a healer of grief, the degree of grief prevalent is probably measurable by the time span of his single state between marriages. Some men are of a tender disposition and welcome being consoled. Others have a reclusive personality and seek no pity. Therefore their grief is not as evident. It is good to console ourselves that our departed ones cannot come to us, but we anticipate going to them. I am glad that my companion shared his dreams of seeing his former companion. I, too, saw her in my dreams at times.

Meeting the spiritual needs of a minister companion must not be neglected. He needs prayer support first of all. There needs to be a oneness in Bible-based convictions. He needs encouragement in boldly and faithfully fulfilling God's call to preach the Word.

Constructive criticism can and should be an asset to a minister husband. When he seeks your advice and counsel, then be honest. When the criticism is unsolicited you need to be especially kind and tactful. Sometimes the counsel can be presented in question form.

We aid him, too, when we unselfishly allow him to be used to aid the spiritual needs of others in personal and evangelistic endeavors. There are times when it is needful to stay at home while he is gone on a preaching mission, whereas at other times the need is best fulfilled by going along.

Of no less consideration is the situation where children are involved. Here again situations vary. If the children are all quite young, Number Two is the only mother they know and accept her as such, which is probably the most ideal.

If the children are all grown, and some are married or away from home, they may find it hard to accept Number Two as Mother. If they cannot accept her, a feeling of aloofness will hinder good communication. When not all live under the same roof, there is not the constant need to fit into and accept each other's lives. Unfortunately, there may be a strained relationship when the family *does* meet.

Perhaps the most crucial situation is when the ages of the children range from old enough to remember Mother to some having left the nest. For some of them it may be hard to understand how their father could love another to the extent of marrying her. To some of them it is so good to have a mother again that their acceptance has minor reservations. Others may be apprehensive of this new mother until she has proved herself worthy of their love.

There is adjusting on the part of each family member. An awareness of this is essential for each member lest any one menber imagines himself to be the only one making these adjustments. When children accept the fact that Daddy needs a companion, they will more readily support and adjust to another mother in the home.

Children should be encouraged to speak of their mother. Number Two needs to assure them that she is not offended when they freely talk about her. This helped me to learn their mother's traits and characteristics which were an aid in mothering. The children should not expect a duplicate of their mother, but they do have a right to expect genuine love and concern from their second mother.

How does Number Two cope with the tremendous responsibility at hand, not being a mother, yet being a mother? "The eternal God is thy refuge, and underneath are the everlasting arms . . ." (Deut. 33:27a). See also Proverbs 3:5,6. As a child by faith looks to her parents for guidance and having needs supplied so she implores the Lord for guidance in the seemingly impossible. My prayer has often been, "Lord, give me those mother feelings and mother qualities. Help me to be a true help, *meet* for my companion."

Another asset for me was observing real mothers. Their speech, manner of conduct in their own life, and in communicating to their children was an aid not only in mothering but also in grandmothering.

Then there is coping with the awareness of being watched by others. They watch how this newlywed handles her new position as wife and mother. This may take awhile to completely overcome, but as she is assured that she is meant for this position, she can confidently carry out her obligations without regarding the keen eyes of others. It is best not to try to be the former spouse, for it never works to try to be someone you are not.

I appreciated much that my husband didn't constantly remind me of his former companion's way of doing things. He accepted me as I was, yet gave constructive criticism, at times, in a loving manner. Being aware that the older children probably have the harder struggle in accepting Number Two, behooves us to have an unselfish yieldedness for the good of the children.

It is good to learn and accommodate the family's tastes and interests. Keep home furnishings as their mother had them, at least until the others agree to rearrange or make changes.

Stepping into a ready-made family may mean dropping some views concerning marriage and child training. Some of Number Two's views may already be established in the family, in an even better outworking than thought possible, while other views are not acceptable in her situation. She must accept the child training and patterns already established. There are definite advantages to be married to one who has paved the way.

What about the many friends an older maiden lady usually has? One cannot "run" with them on a regular basis and at the same time do justice to her role as wife and mother. To forget or ignore them need not be. After making the family's friends your friends and their interests your interests, invite your friends into your home. Give your children the privilege of making new acquaintances and broadening their friendships. Being wholeheartedly engaged in homemaking for your companion and children supersedes some of the former seemingly selfish activities engaged in.

What about making decisions? Before marriage a single person seeks the Lord in all matters at hand, large or small. She is, in accordance with I Cor. 7:32-34, concerned with how she may please the Lord. Now suddenly, after years of making decisions alone with the Lord she is confronted with presenting matters to her husband as well.

Many times she finds it helpful and a real source of security to be able to counsel and reach a decision with someone who loves her and cares for her. At other times it brings a struggle, especially when his decisions differ from what she would have felt the Lord wanted her to do. She must return again to I Corinthians and consider how she may please her husband, recognizing the Lord's command to submit in reverence.

Are you given to much traveling? Be ready to accept that much of the traveling you do after marriage could be related to church work. For us, many miles have been traveled to our mission in Belize. Occasionally, there will be a trip especially to Number Two's personal choosing. We have been taking special trips, some years, for our wedding anniversary. We may visit some shut-in in another state or locality or include some business, thus making it not purely a pleasure trip, but enjoyable.

It is essential that Number Two and her companion are all alone periodically. First marriages need solitude at times; how much more when entering marriage into a ready-made family. Number Two needs to find time (and her companion should realize this) to discuss things that need to be discussed in the absence of children. In first-time marriages there is the advantage of discussing any and everything at meal time or whenever, as long as the children are small and don't understand.

When decisions concerning the rest of the family need to be made, discuss the situation together alone and then present it to the family. This is especially necessary when the children have not all accepted their new mother and may be averse to most suggestions she makes.

If a strained atmosphere prevails between a child or children and Number Two, it needs to be searched out and proper steps taken to restore communication. Frustrations are likely to exist at times, but need not be normal if we are sensitive to each other's welfare.

Acknowledging shortcomings and mistakes and asking forgiveness goes a long way in maintaining proper relationships. The story is told of a second marriage where the wife reported their happy marriage. The secret for it was that her husband freely acknowledged and apologized for his mistakes. When asked about her response to her own mistakes, she replied, "I haven't come to that place yet." Let this never be true of Christ's followers.

Another encounter Number Two faces is, Will the children be *his* children or *our* children? For us it was settled before marriage that we will speak of *our* children. Perhaps it is more perplexing or embarrassing for others as some people do ask about *his* children, but that can easily be overlooked.

Is Number Two worthy of the Mother title? Some would say definitely not; that they could not call another person Mother. In our experience, we decided before marriage that a different term would be used than was used for the children's mother. Instead of "Mommy" my title would be "Mother." The children were informed of this. This was not an easy transition for the children and came about gradually for some of them. However, the Mother title challenges me to live up to that name.

After thirteen years of married life, there is still that feeling of unworthiness of the title when the children address me "Mother." It just really makes me want to be the best mother I possibly can be, though I'm a Number Two and still learning.

About the Writer

The Wilford Stutzman family has been involved in missions for many years. On one such return trip the family met with a tragic accident which claimed the lives of Mother and two children. This left Father and eight children.

Brother Wilford was ordained Deacon in 1951 and Bishop in 1970 in the Salem Mennonite Church.

On October 25, 1975 Wilford and Eunice (Miller) were united in Holy Matrimony. They are continuing their mission endeavors in Belize and now have several married children and their familes on the Mission Field.

Wilford is a farmer and Eunice is busy being Mother and Grandmother and enjoys piecing quilts as a hobby. They reside at Keota, Iowa.

If you would reap praise,
You must sow the seeds,
Gentle words and
Useful deed.

Blessing For The Middle Aged

Happy is the couple where God is the center and where the Spirit of Christ rules.

Happy is the couple who welcome their children and grandchildren and each is given his rightful place.

Happy is the couple who are involved in the work of the church and worship regularly together.

Happy is the couple who put the other's happiness first.

Happy is the couple who show their love in ways that mean the most to the other.

Happy is the couple who each seeks to bring out the best in the other and to show his own best self at all times.

Happy is the couple when their children grow up and they as grownups do not act like children.

Happy is the couple who have the assurance of their heavenly home.

—Selected and adapted by AB

A Late Start

by Lizzie (Mrs. Yost) Miller

My husband and I were well into middle age when we were married. Having a late start may have some advantages, but there are also some disadvantages.

One disadvantage is that, out of necessity, a single woman must learn to think and act independently to a large extent. Because of that, I found it hard to adjust to the fact that I was not the one in charge when a major decision needed to be made. It would have been easier if I had recognized from the beginning that I was not in command; and, regardless of what followed the decision, it was not my responsibility, but my husband's. This does not mean taking an "I don't care" attitude, but rather placing my husband in his rightful position.

It was not until independency was relinquished that I could experience the blessing of being a true "helpmeet." Yes, it is a blessing to meet those who come to our door from both far and near because of my husband's ministry. It is a blessing to do added cooking and washing. The Lord generously provides. It is a blessing that my minister husband chooses to spill out to me his concerns, griefs, and triumphs. It is a blessing to pray together and sometimes laugh together. It is a blessing when he shares confidential things that need to stay confidential. It is also a blessing to pray for him when he needs to make decisions, and when he preaches.

Not only was there a change from being single to becoming a minister's wife, but there was also an introduction into a different church fellowship. The well-prepared sermons, the good congregational singing, and the over-all teaching program is a tremendous blessing. I have come to love and cherish this fellowship.

However, I see some distress signals. Why is the admonition of the church leaders taken so lightly? The lack of uniformity has affected our witness. A young girl who came to our home was contemplating joining the New Order Amish Church. She felt rather handicapped in doing without a car, but when I asked her why she doesn't think about our fellowship she had a ready answer. "Your people are edging into the world." A young mother from a non-Mennonite background, but a member of our fellowship in a neighboring state, told me it grieves them to see some of us head in the direction they came from.

We have become a prosperous people. Money comes easily, therefore our minds are turning to "things." What is more conducive to creating materialistic thinking, than frequent trips to the shopping mall? Has shopping become a means of entertainment?

There is hope. Our God is still on the throne. He is the Almighty One, the Just One, the Gracious One. He has said, "If my people, which are called by my name, shall humble themselves, and pray, and seek my face, and turn from their wicked ways; then will I hear from heaven, and will forgive their sin, and will heal their land."

About the Writer

Born in Plain City, Ohio, Lizzie Yoder grew up in a family of five brothers and three sisters.

She enjoyed her single life and was in service at Red Lake, Canada, for several years.

In 1975, Yost's first wife died of cancer and a year later, Yost and Lizzie were united in marriage.

Together they are known for their concern for the churches as a whole. Yost is bishop of the Bethel Church in Berlin, Ohio.

Lizzie has "inherited" six children and together they enjoy their grandchildren.

She enjoys quilting and keeps busy when Yost is busy with church work.

To The Bereaved

Hovering o'er my head
    Lowering fast
Is this gray cloud I see,
    Daylight has passed.
Engulfed in solemn gloom
    Standing alone,
No one to share my grief
    At Heaven's throne?

Ah, yes, I feel a hand
    Clasping my own,
Whispering heartening words
    Stifling my groan.
Beyond the thickest clouds
    There still is blue,
Though shadows shroud me now,
    His love is True.

Thank God for faithful friends
    Whose hearts are touched.
Encouragements and prayers
    In grief means much.
Comfort, a healing balm,
    Peace in the heart,
Helps soothe what death has wrought
    When loved ones part.

Thank God for grief's dread work
    For tears that come.
To mellow and fit me
    For Home, my Home.

—*Miriam L. Druist*

Coping With Grief
Interviews and Observations
by Aaron Jr. and Marion Lapp

S everal years ago a man who stopped by our farm told me of many troubles a friend of his has had. He said his friend was so distraught and really was at the end of the rope. So he told his friend to tie a knot and hang on. Is there nothing better to offer a friend?

Material for this chapter does not come from personal experience. A bit of this writing may come from observation. Most of it is from interviews with three widows (one had been married to a deacon and two to bishops).

Our first interview is with Mrs. Malinda Stoltzfus, widow of Allen Lee Stoltzfus. He was ordained deacon at the Pequea Amish Mennonite Church of Lancaster County, Pennsylvania in January, 1982. He passed away in November, 1986, not having served quite five years in the ministry.

Writer: "Malinda, would you care to share with us about your experience as a widow of a deacon?"

Malinda: "God and His grace is the Source of all comfort. He makes one able to work through the shock, the acceptance of such a sudden turn in one's plans. God's people are a resource for continuing that needed support in

205

my spirit and soul. By accepting me, my friends help me work through accepting all this as God's perfect plan.

"The first night after we learned the doctor's diagnosis of Allen's condition was the hardest time for our family. One son said, 'Mom, you always said life isn't fair. Do you also say it isn't just?' 'No,' I said. 'Life may not always seem fair, but God is fair. He is right in all He does. Our vision is often too short-sighted to see His over-all plan.' "

Writer: "Out of the role of a deacon's wife what do you miss most since your husband is not here?"

Malinda; "I was only at the annual church-wide Ministers' Meeting three times. I also miss attending the local ministers' meeting. But most of all I miss the visits we made together to our church families. Visiting was something we did quite frequently. I don't go myself to make these visits. So much of life is just not the same any more."

Writer: "Do you have anyone else with a similiar experience near your age to share with and confide in?"

Malinda: "No, not really."

Writer: "Besides housekeeping and routine lawn and garden work, do you have special projects or 'outside' work?"

Malinda: "Well, yes, I've been trying to be helpful to supply others' needs. I teach a young mother's Sunday school class. I wrote letters of reply to people who wrote to me after Allen's passing. I send a lot of cards to various people. Every Tuesday I work at the Brandywine Hospital on a volunteer basis. That is good for me. Our son Ed was there five days as a patient. Ed and Allen were both there for out-patient services."

Ed and Allen both had cancer at the same time, but not the same kind of cancer. Ed's case was diagnosed before his father. (But Allen passed away eleven months before Ed.)

Writer: "At what times do you most sense the loss of your husband?"

Malinda: "This may occur at various times. But I feel it most on my way to church. The change is very substantial. Finding my place in the church is a big adjustment."

Writer: "What part of your routine at home is most difficult for you?"

Malinda: "Making meals is my hardest thing. Just three years ago there were six people at our table. Everything was so wonderful. I enjoyed my house, my kitchen, planning and preparing meals. Now it is only my son Nate and me. Aden was married and then Frieda. Nate plans to be married next month. Then I will move off the farm to living quarters adjacent to my parents' house.

"Allen's favorite dessert was shoo-fly cake. After Allen had been gone a year, I hadn't made it once. The family said I should make it again, keep on making my specialties."

Writer: "Did you make it since then?"

Malinda: "No, Allen isn't here to tell me how good it is."

Writer: "How has God sustained you and supplied for you?"

Malinda: "I don't know how. I just know He has and does. I personally will to accept Him for all He says He is, and for what He promises to do. He is my safety and my security. Our God is fair, and He is faithful.

"When Allen became sick, in my mind I asked 'Why now? Why now after being in the ministry for less than five years. Why . . .?' But 'why' is the wrong question. Asking 'why' leads to a dead end street. Or into a tunnel without an exit at some distant point.

"Rather than asking 'why,' God wants me to ask 'how' and 'what.' 'Lord, how do You want me to respond? What do You want me to learn and do?' 'How' and 'what' lead somewhere. With that there is progress for now and for the future.

"I have been given to see where Allen's and Ed's testimonies in suffering and death have been the means of some being saved. Their lives touched certain people that others could not reach."

Writer: "What else has been unique in your experience?"

Malinda: "You would think after you learn your spouse has only a few months to live it would come natural to talk about death and how I should do as a widow. Not so. Spontaneous talk about the end, the consequent changes and adjustments hardly happens. You almost must make it happen. It wasn't easy to face the facts. For Allen it meant facing the reality of meeting God and leaving me alone, a widow, and the children fatherless. It was actually hard to plan for the end and thereafter. But we did talk about it some. We were advised to spend lots of time together. It was in those unplanned, unstructured times that we would talk about the future."

Writer: "What would you say to widows of ministers?"

Malinda: "Support the ministers and their wives as the work of the church goes on without your direct involvement. Bad feelings and suspicious ideas can creep in and spoil previously good relationships. Someone else was ordained deacon in Allen's stead. I can very well accept the Lord's choice and give my support to the new deacon and his wife. Failure to accept all these changes can cause one to be bitter toward the church and even toward God.

"Be open to other avenues of service and activity. I've been so busy since I'm a widow. God has poured His grace into my life and is filling the empty and lonely places with Himself."

Our second interview is with Amanda, widow of the late Roman Miller, bishop of the Hartville Conservative (non-conference) Church of Hartville, Ohio for 42 years (1936-1978). She has been a good friend of our family for many years.

On their wedding day Amanda was 24, Roman 27. At age 31 he was ordained to the ministry, and to the office of bishop a little less than a year later. He led a very active life at home and often away from home in the work of the church. Here is her testimony.

"In the nearly fifty years of marriage, our lives were continually intertwined with the work of the ministry. Its struggles and triumphs caused our lives to be blended in a special bond of closeness. Roman did the administrating, the preaching, but my investment of support on his behalf made it seem as though a part of me was invisibly there beside him.

"I miss the special meetings. Hearing him speak to the church and seeing how he handled problem situations was a sense of fulfillment to me. Others would tell me how touching his manners and speaking were at weddings, baptisms, and communion services.

"After Roman passed away it was hard for me to go into Roman's study. I was in shock so long—I don't know how long. The adjustment to widowhood was not easy. Life seemed reduced so drastically. Going back to Florida was hardest of all. Some people would say, 'And who are you?' (Wanting to be a woman under God with a personal identity is no doubt every widow's delight and right.) The shortest route to identifying myself was to say 'Roman

Miller was my husband.' But some would say 'Who *were* you?" (As though in the past she was somebody but now is something less.) Then I would say 'I was Roman Miller's wife.' 'Oh yes, Roman's wife. Yes, we knew Roman.'

"Roman kept such careful and meticulous records. He traveled a good bit for church conferences, special meetings, helping new fellowship churches get started, and other various church work. We almost never went on vacation. Roman took church work so seriously—that would come first. When our children were older, they would say, 'Dad, we think you should take time off and go on a trip.' A number of times he would say, 'Yes, sometime we want to go on a trip west . . . .' But that never happened.

"In the circles where I move the other ministers' wives are much younger. They would graciously invite me to come to their activities, but I didn't feel I fitted socially. Somehow I concluded I wouldn't belong.

"Loneliness is one of the most real feelings I have. This isn't because I have nothing to do. There *is* much to do—there is enough to occupy what gift and energies I yet have. Loneliness is most acute on Sundays, especially in the evening.

"One time I overheard someone ask one of our sons 'How's Mother doing?' 'Oh, she's doing real well,' he replied. 'She is a strong woman, you know. Really committed.' My heart sank. I said within myself, 'Don't you know how alone I feel, how I despair at times?'

"In those first years as a widow, some people would have so many words to say, but people's kind deeds and frequent visits have meant, and still mean, the most to me. Sometimes I felt hurt by not being included, other times when I was invited I felt too grieved to go. (Maybe we need to invite widows and tell them we'll stop in and take them along.) I liked hearing people talk of Roman's life for then I knew they missed him too. When they didn't I was tempted to think they don't even miss him.

"At first I prayed much for a new life of personal serving and giving. Slowly I found people and places where I could make a meaningful contribution of myself. Every morning I pray, 'Lord there must be something I can do for You today.' Now there is so much to do for people in Jesus' name. Somehow God saw to it that I would have no financial need for these years. There is a special joy in sharing with ministers and the needy. I mail cards and tracts to children in the church at various times. As God brings people to my mind I send them a note and tract.

"I remind myself to look on the bright side. People don't want to hear my sob story. So I just praise the Lord over and over again to myself and to others. After sharing life together with a good, faithful, minister husband, parting will be painful, but one doesn't need to major in that grief.

"God loves me—I am secure in Him. He is faithful and He answers prayer."

The third interview was with Edna, widow of Elam Kauffman. He served in the ministry at the Weavertown Amish Mennonite Church in Lancaster County, Pennsylvania, for 45 years. Twenty of those years were as bishop. Edna is also my (Aaron) much loved mother-in-law. Her testimony follows.

"I suppose no one really can fully prepare for widowhood. The loss of one's dearest on earth is an incalculable loss. But God's grace is always sufficient and is granted *as* needs arise, not before.

"Elam and I traveled many miles in various responsibilities for the church. Some experiences were sad with various trials and testings. However, most of our encounters with other people and churches were times of rich blessing under God. We gained many wonderful friends over the years.

"Since Elam's passing, things have changed drastically. I have the blessed thought that he served his generation. My life goes on—alone, and yet not alone. I have good, helpful neighbors. I find resource from the church people by their prayers and words of encouragement. Things that are given and visits with me are a continual means of blessing. The support of my children is a constant source of encouragement.

"I do miss the fellowship with other minister couples. Being with such was our greatest joy. And then I miss my children and grandchildren who live far away. One lives elsewhere in Pennsylvania, one in Belize and one in Brazil. But it is reassuring to see my children walk in truth and be ready to serve God wherever He calls.

"People say time heals. Well, yes, to a certain extent. On special days like Father's Day or his birthday or the anniversary of his death there are tugs at the affection and memories. Would one want to lose all such affection and blot out the memories? Of course not! To be sure, there is a certain longing for those good times. But one should not spoil the present with wishing to live in the past. I would not want to burden others with my grief all over again. So I seek to live in the present with a view of the future.

"I believe my husband's parting was God's will by His divine timing. Who am I to refuse and resist God's decree and arrangement? If I can't accept God's doings in death as well as in life, how could I claim God's promises?

"God is a personal Being to me, His Word is true and His promises are precious. I claim these promises in a special way—'I will never leave thee nor forsake thee.' 'He careth for you.' 'All things work together for good . . .'

"Some ways I occupy my time in, sewing for others at home, and helping at our church sewing circle. I enjoy reading church newsletters and periodicals as well as the Bible. I follow with interest who is on the mission field and what is happening there.

"Time goes on, things change and issues change. But the same forces are at work as were for generations. Satan tries to disrupt the good. But Jesus is building His church, and in some way I want to continue to be a part of that for His glory until He comes."

Now back to our friend holding on at the end of the rope. The sufficiency of Christ to sustain us is not in how well we hold on to Him. No, no, no! Much rather, He is entirely sufficient to meet our unique and special needs as well as our daily needs according to how we trust in Him. To trust Him also means to wait on Him. For it is really He who holds us—not we who hold on to Him. In Jesus we find our Solace, our Succor, our Supply for every need. For he is our all in all.

About the Writers

Aaron Jr. and Marian Lapp are life-long residents of Lancaster County, Pennsylvania, who like the farm and love the church. Marian's father, Elam Kauffman, was ordained before Marian was born. The Lapps and their seven children were born and raised in the Weavertown Church.

Since 1973 Aaron has taught a three-week term at Calvary Bible School every year except 1987. He has served on the CBS Board since 1984, as Vice-Chairman 1985-1988, and Chairman 1989-_____. In December, 1981, he was ordained deacon of the Weavertown Church, frequently conducts Christian finance seminars, is a contributing editor to *Calvary Messenger* and is writing a series of articles on the *Christian Financial Outlook*.

He has interviewed three widows and penned the above article, with Marian's assistance and counsel.

No one can safely
go abroad
who does not find
contentment
to stay at home.

Totally Available

Totally available, hear now my humble prayer
Totally available to Jesus anywhere
Totally available I give myself anew
Totally available the will of God to do.

Totally available my life with Him is sealed
Totally available each hour to Him I yield
Totally available this is the song I sing
Totally available to Jesus Christ my King.

—David Gorden McIntyre

The Mission Field . . . Our Home and Career

by Esther (Mrs. David) Herschberger

While on vacation, I attended a ladies' sewing circle. As we were quilting, I said something about going home the next day. "So the North is home?" someone asked. Without hesitation, I said "Yes." But it hasn't always been that way. Twenty-four years ago I couldn't have said that. Somewhere along the way, Canada has changed from being "away from home" to being "at home."

When I was about twelve years old, I remember telling my mother that I thought I would be a missionary some day. Years later I learned that she had that earnest desire as a young mother, but never got to go. Instead she served faithfully as a minister's wife for more than thirty-five years and saw most of their nine children active in voluntary service or as longer-term missionaries. She encouraged my aspiration, and when it became a reality, she and my father willingly let me go, first as a single person and later with my husband and family. In the many years since that, when coming home on furlough and then going again, I don't recall that my parents ever made us feel like we should come home to stay and not be so far from home. I thank the Lord for that! It meant a lot to us to have their blessing on what we felt was God's will for our lives.

217

It wasn't easy to go, especially when we left for Canada and realized it may be for long-term service. I can still remember that lonely feeling many years ago when we were driving those last 300 miles over dusty roads to our new home. I felt we were getting farther and farther away from everything that was familiar and dear to us. Somehow it seemed so permanent, such a "no-turning-back" situation. There were only the four of us, my husband, our two pre-schoolers and myself.

We arrived at our new home, and everything was so strange to us. No familar faces anywhere! The nearest missionary family lived 90 miles away. I missed my dear family very much. As the letters started to come, telling of family gatherings, weddings, funerals and church events, it tugged at my heart and many times the tears flowed. One day I was so lonely for my sister. That night I dreamed I saw her and had a good visit. The next day my loneliness was gone! Praise the Lord! I knew He understood and would keep on meeting my need.

Time also has a way of transforming the strange and unfamiliar surroundings into "home." Gradually the people who were just so many new faces became our friends, and we felt ourselves becoming a part of our new community.

What a blessing and comfort our children were to us those first months and years as we adapted to our new home. However, as they got older, we sometimes wondered if it was fair for them to be so isolated, and whether we should be here permanently. Twice we left for a year's leave of absence to evaluate our life-style and career and to determine the Lord's further will for us. This also gave the children a chance to be with relatives and to identify with a larger church group. Both times it seemed right to our family to return to our place of service.

But what is it really like to raise a family in a culture other than what you were used to? Is it advisable or even possible? It can be very difficult. Children, along with their parents, can have lonely times away from relatives and close friends and being with people who don't understand them and have a different value system. For our children it often meant standing alone in the public school when questionable activities were in session. Our children were expected to be model Christians when they were attacked verbally or physically and all their childish nature wanted to react otherwise. It also meant trying hard to be all- Canadian and not let the other students find out you are from the States. They saw much evil in the community and heard of violence and tragic deaths of people they knew well.

However, it's not all negative. Having children grow up in a different environment has many blessings and added bonuses! Learning to relate cross-culturally when you are young can be a real asset. Some of our children have found this helpful as they became involved in voluntary service elsewhere and had to relate to yet another culture. Seeing the change in people's lives when they become Christians has been an advantage too. This helps children develop a burden for the unsaved at an early age.

Because of isolation, a missionary family tends to be more home-centered. Our whole family life revolves around our home. Sure, we have callers, unexpected guests, children playing in the yard and activities in our basement. But it's all at our house and the family is together. This was especially true when the children were younger. We also spent a lot of quality family time going on picnics, camping, traveling at vacation time and "just talking." Family night and individual birthday picnics with their dad were highlights too. We found out that confidences that are usually shared with peers and close friends are more likely to be shared with parents and help build closeness and security.

The question that disturbs every conscientious missionary is, "How can I spend adequate time in my ministry, but not neglect my family?" Probably every Christian parent is concerned about this, whether you are a missionary or whether you have a regular job. In many ways the work for the wife and the mother is the same. We cook, clean, sew, do laundry and care for our family. But in addition to that, we share deeply in our husband's work of sharing the Gospel and meeting the needs of hurting people. We are faced daily with so many possibilities of ministry! How can we do justice to everything?

First and foremost to remember is our need to maintain a vital fellowship with the Lord. Isaiah 40:31 has been a favorite verse of mine for many years. "They that wait upon the Lord shall renew their strength. . ." I thank the Lord for my husband who encouraged me to periodically spend several hours at a quiet place away from home to replenish my spiritual reservoir. This was especially valuable during the time when the children were small and daily quiet time was often interrupted.

I've also learned that my work doesn't always have to be done at a certain time and in a certain way. Some things I planned to do, don't have to be done at all! When visitors are coming for a week, I try to have things in order when they come and then let things slide until they leave. I don't put on "company" meals all the time. For me, it's more important to enjoy the fellowship than to try to be the perfect cook and housekeeper with a house full of people.

Some missionary mothers would rather spend all their time in domestic duties and gladly leave the ministry part to their husbands and fellow-workers. Others are eager to get out where the action is and tend to neglect the home and family. Somehow we need to find the correct balance.

Much of a mother's ministry can be right at home with her children. We had sewing classes, Bible Clubs for children, Bible Studies,—and callers, right in our two-bedroom house! For several years we kept short-term foster children. Our children loved it! For many activities, we shouldn't wait "until the children are older." We won't have the energy then! And the opportunities may be gone.

It's important to include our children as much as possible in our activities, then they won't feel neglected. If they see us happy and enjoying our ministry, they probably will enjoy it too. David often took a child along to the Indian Reserve on Sunday afternoon when he went to have a church service. Sometimes I took a child along when I visited a new mother. Our children took a special liking for old people and formed some lasting friendships. They still like to go see them when they come home to visit. One of our boys was asked to be pall-bearer at the funeral of such a friend. They developed a spiritual burden for some and witnessed to them many times. One old lady accepted the Lord.

A very important part of a wife's ministry is to be willing to let her husband go and minister while she stays at home. Many times David needed to be away from home for a few days or longer. When the children were small, I tried to have things continue in routine as much as possible. During family prayers, we always asked God for safety and blessings on Daddy. David traveled a lot by boat and one time a son prayed that "Daddy wouldn't fall in the water and be swallowed by a whale like Jonah!" It was important to help the children know that what their dad is doing is important and that he is away because he loves God and wants to help other people to know God. It's amazing how children will accept a situation if the mother can keep from feeling sorry for herself and the children. Then it is also easier for the father to go.

In conclusion, I will say that missionary life isn't easy and there are difficulties in raising a family in such an environment. But no other place is easy either. Life isn't meant to be comfortable, but it can be very good as we follow the Lord. The important thing is that we are at the place He wants us to be. Whether we are in our homeland or on foreign soil, we need to have a purpose in being where we are. We were created to glorify God and proclaim Him. "Reverence for God gives a man deep strength; his children have a place of refuge and security" (Prov. 14:26, Taylor's Paraphrase).

About the Writer

Esther's father was a dedicated minister who encouraged his children to put God first in their lives.

Soon after their marriage in March 22, 1959, David and Esther Herschberger answered the call to the far North, where they have been faithfully serving the Indians over the past 25 years.

Their family of five children and their personal lives have been a challenge to many that "Home" can be in a foreign country and not merely in a fine house.

They reside at Hudson, a mission outreach in Ontario.

Some of Esther's hobbies are reading and piecing quilts.

Folded Hands

To serve with folded hands
    May be the harder part
For you who keep faith strong
    And constant in your heart.

To serve with folded hands
    Requires strength of mind
To overcome despair
    And lasting courage find.

To serve with folded hands
    Will bring a rich reward;
For folded hands may point
    A sure way to the Lord.

—*Allen D. Mack*

Adjusting To Life As A Returned Missionary

by Amanda (Mrs. Roman) Mullet

A t first glance I misread this title, "Adjusting to life as a *retarded* missionary."

Retarded persons (or rather brain-injured) often have difficulty expressing themselves. They often find it difficult to understand others, and vice versa, people often have difficulty understanding them. Many times I have felt just like that! Is it your fault? Is it my fault? I'm not blaming you —and please do not blame me.

We return with our lives torn betwixt two. We are so delighted to come "home," but what about those needy souls and friends we just left, and the culture we finally adapted to there? "Home" is so different from when we had left it seven years ago. Small children are now school children, school children are now youth, youth are now married and old people are still older—or have passed on. Homes are more elaborate (to us extremely elaborate) in comparison with where we came from,—and on—and on—. So what am I experiencing? A culture shock? Yes, a culture shock in returning home.

So if you see missionary families or individuals returning home, please accept them for what they are. You may not understand, but they very much need your support in their readjustment to life at home. Examples:

The returned missionary couple with children also has a great responsibility to help the children meet their needs in a different environment. Here the "home" folks can also be of great help. It may be that the children (unless surrounded with family members) will not be so readily accepted the first while, due to their time of absence. Children will soon detect this and may become quite discouraged.

Parental alertness to this can be of great help. Plan special activities for them, like fishing, picnicking, etc. Shopping together would also provide an interesting way to observe and discuss contrasts between the foreign country and home. But most of all they need contact with other children, lest they withdraw themselves and further complicate the difficulty of adjustment.

Ultimately, what is my perspective to modern gadgets? Before our return from a very poor country, I felt even though we will be living amongst the wealthy (compared to El Salvador), when we return home I would still prefer a "pila" to do hand washing, and cement tile floor instead of rugs. Why did I feel this way? Because I was living amongst the poor who live the simple life—"and I was one of them." Since I am home again, my perspective to modern gadgets has changed.

In the work we are engaged in now, what would I do without an automatic washer, and a dryer, or the microwave to cook a meal in a few minutes when time is limited? Incidentally, I also have a carpet plus a good vacuum sweeper. As a returned missionary, I need to keep my priorities straight, and be a faithful steward of that which I am allowed. "Moreover, it is required in stewards that a man be found faithful" (I Cor. 4:2).

Seven years on the mission field is not long, but now,

fourteen years later, I am still in the process of catching up. I have blessed memories of those few short years in a needy foreign land, with people who are my brothers and sisters in Christ.

ᘉᓚ

About The Writer

Roman and Amanda Mullet were married December 31, 1942 and are considered "spiritual parents" to many. Roman was one of the first ministers to pioneer the Beachy Amish churches in Holmes County, Ohio 31 years ago.

They served almost seven years as missionaries in El Salvador and then they returned to the United States. He pastored the small church at Mission Home, Virginia for 10 years.

Now since 1987 they have accepted the call to organize seminars at Penn Valley Christian Retreat—a long dreamed of vision that has become reality.

They have 5 children and they too, are active in mission and church related work.

Amanda find fulfillment in assisting her husband in the office plus being a homemaker. She enjoys quilting as a hobby.

A Faithful Daughter-In-Law

"Entreat me not to leave you,
Or to turn back
from following after you;
For wherever you go, I will go;
And wherever you lodge, I will lodge;
Your people shall be my people,
And your God, my God.
Where you die, I will die,
And there will I be buried.
The Lord do so to me, and more also,
If anything but death
parts you and me."

—*Ruth 1:16, 17, NKJ*

Mother/Daughter-In-Law Relationships

by Delilah (Mrs. Urie) Sharp

F annie was a beautiful young woman who grew up in a well-to-do Mennonite home, with every possible financial advantage. Her parents spent much time away from home due to work and social obligations and had little time for her. Consequently Fannie was insecure.

When Fannie married Ralph, who came from a very close-knit family, she resented the closeness between Ralph and his mother. As Fannie's security was in Ralph, she felt threatened when she didn't have him to herself. During their rare visits to his folks, Fannie sulked instead of entering into the conversation and activities. Her reaction caused tension and frustration in his parents' home.

Ralph's mother was devastated, not knowing what to do to help matters. Ralph was caught between his wife and his mother, the two people he loved most dearly. He was hesitant to spend much time with his family because of Fannie's jealousy. And yet, Ralph longed for the good chats his family used to have before his marriage.

God intended families to live in harmony and peace. What is more beautiful than to see a family unit working together: father, mother, son, daughter, in-laws, and grand-children.

God gives us directives for every area of our life. He is especially concerned with our relationships within the family. He wants us to live harmoniously. "Follow peace with all men, and holiness, without which no man shall see the Lord" (Heb. 12:14). "And be at peace among your-selves" (I Thess. 5:13). "Live in peace; and the God of love and peace shall be with you" (II Cor. 13:11).

In the Book of Ruth we have a beautiful example of a mother and daughter-in-law who had a lovely relationship. Naomi was a caring and unselfish person who put the welfare of her in-laws above her own desires. This is evident when she released them to return to their families. But the bond between Ruth and Naomi was too strong to be easily severed. Ruth committed herself to Naomi and Naomi's God. Because she won the respect and devotion of her daughter-in-law, Naomi lived many happy years with Ruth. In Ruth 4:15 it is clearly stated that Ruth was better to Naomi than seven sons!

Establishing this kind of relationship is not easy, and takes a humble spirit, a ready acceptance of each other; giving and taking.

Here are a few suggestions on how we as parents can prepare our children to have good in-law relationships.

1) Lead them to a deep personal relationship with God. This is the foundation for all other relationships.

2) Make sure they feel secure in our parental love.

3) Help them to develop a good self-image, realizing that they are what they are because of God's working. We have nothing in ourselves to be proud of. A person who does not feel good about herself, and does not accept herself for the way God made her, will not feel good about

others, especially not her in-laws.

4) Having love and unity with your husband sets a beautiful example.

5) Start early in building a close, warm relationship with your daughters, helping them to relate to other family members, grandparents and the larger family, as well as with the church. Establishing close family relationships lays a firm foundation for the difficult experiences and tests later. Show an interest in their friends, encouraging them to bring home the ones you approve.

6) Be there when they need you. Sometimes our children feel we are too busy to bother with their problems and struggles. Young people are often ready to talk after coming home from an evening of activity. You may be too tired, but it may be your best opportunity for a heart-to-heart talk.

7) Teach your children the seriousness of dating and what to look for in a marriage partner. Be open, frank, and sincerely interested in their questions.

8) Above all, pray for them "without ceasing," praying God's protection over them.

Remember, our enemy is out to destroy family relationships, including mother/daughter-in-law relationships.

James was attracted to Diane, a lovely young girl from his church. Before he dated, he asked his parents' opinion of her.

During their three years of dating, James often took her to his home where they spent many happy hours with his family. They played games, shared ideas, sometimes munching popcorn, sitting around the table with the family. Diane was included in a number of family projects.

Long before they talked about marriage, James' family learned to love Diane. And Diane felt at home, accepted and loved by the whole family.

When James asked his parents' advice about marriage, there was already a feeling that Diane belonged.

After the engagement, James' mother offered to help where needed with the wedding, the new home, or whatever. She was careful not to give too many suggestions or be too nosey, but was ready to help when Diane asked for counsel. Today there is a deep love and closeness between Diane and her mother-in-law. The reason is obvious.

ༀ

During engagement and the first years of marriage the young couple faces many decisions and adjustments. They need to feel the interest and support of the parents as they make important decisions.

Each partner brings to marriage different traditions, customs, and life styles. Ideally, they choose from the best of both families. Our children must be granted the freedom to choose. We need to learn to let go and not make them feel guilty. It is only as we free them to build their own home, that we truly keep them. We probably won't always agree with their decisions, but we must love them, none the less.

We need mother-love, not smother-love. We must avoid unrealistic expectations. The following illustrates the point:

After John and Becky were married, his mother expected them to come home for dinner every Sunday, and for every special holiday. If they didn't, John's mother freely expressed her displeasure and disappointment. Very quickly negative feelings developed between Becky and her mother-in-law.

Sam and Ruth were married about the same time as John and Becky. Ruth loved to stop in to see Sam's mother. They always had so much to talk about. Ruth felt a genuine love from Sam's mother; an acceptance for who she was and not just because she was Sam's wife. Sam's mother made Ruth feel special. Ruth knew she could always depend on Sam's mother for advice and help. She was not demanding, nor overbearing. This is why Ruth didn't feel threatened by her.

If you as a mother truly care about your son, you will want a good relationship with his wife.

Let us look at a few practical suggestions for mothers-in-law:

- Pray for your daughter-in-law (and family) daily.
- Treat her like a daughter, but a bit more carefully.
- Call her occasionally, but not every day.
- Be there when she needs you, even if it's only to go pick up the car at the garage, or to take her somewhere.
- Ask her for a small favor you know she can do.
- Stop in to chat for a few minutes.
- Praise her for her accomplishments.
- Don't always be giving advice; but be available.
- Never downgrade or talk against her to your son.
- Be careful about always taking your son his favorite foods.
- Compliment her cooking and housekeeping where you can.

- Don't be pushy with your ideas, though your ideas may be right.
- Be a Naomi: put her welfare above your wants.
- Respect their privacy!
- Remember her birthday.
- Discover her likes and dislikes. For instance, if she likes cantaloupes, share one of yours.
- In true humility, be frank with each other. Tell her you want to be her friend; and encourage her to tell you when she doesn't like what you do.

As with any relationship, there may be times when you need to confront each other; but do it with love, knowing and remembering that you want to build, not tear down, relationships. There needs to be a giving and taking by both.

Linda and Larry had met each other at Bible school. After dating several years, they were married and moved into Larry's community. Besides moving far from home, Linda hardly knew anyone. She wanted to be friends with Larry's family.

When asked why she had such a good relationship with Larry's mother, Linda said that because she loved Larry, she resolved to love his mother, too. She determined to accept her mother-in-law for what she was. Instead of picking on her weaknesses, Linda determined to focus on the good qualities of Larry's mother.

Now for a few helpful hints for the new brides like Linda:

- Build on the mother-in-law's good qualities.
- Determine to overlook her faults. (Love covers a multitude of sins.)

- Don't talk against her to your husband. It will only turn him against you.
- Accept, and respect her advice. (Remember Ruth and Naomi.)
- Ask her advice about foods. (Who knows better what your husband likes than his mother?)
- Remember, she's the mother of the one you love; she probably taught him the values you admire in him.
- It will likely please her if you ask an occasional favor ("Do you have a recipe for . . .?" or "Do you think you could . . .?")
- Remember she loves your husband, too. In his infancy she changed his diapers; in his childhood she kissed away tears; all these years she took care of him.
- Pray much about your relationship with her. Ask God to show you your blind spots.
- Be willing to change your schedule when you see your mother-in-law really needs you.
- Make a special effort to involve her in your lives, especially when you live in a different community. Keep her in touch with your family by letters, pictures, and phone calls.
- Resolve to be the best of friends.

In conclusion, a secure woman will understand that the happiness of her husband is a common interest with her mother-in-law, and they will work together to cultivate that happiness. Poor relationships between mother and daughter-in-law can put tremendous stress on marriage relationships—can even wreck marriages. On the other hand, a beautiful relationship between in-laws, helps to build warm relationships in the larger family: a beautiful testimony and example for many generations to come.

Let's be the best in-laws in town!

ᘒ

About the Writer

Delilah's father, Roman H. Miller, was ordained three days before she was born. From early childhood she has known life in a minister and bishop's home, and is now a minister's wife. She is a lifelong resident of Hartville, Ohio. Delilah taught school four years before marrying Urie Sharp of Belleville, PA, in June of 1959. During most of the last 30 years, Urie has been teaching at Hartville Christian School. He was ordained to the ministry in May, 1963. Their family consists of five children and three grandchildren.

The family has been involved with missions for about twenty-five years. Urie has been a member of Mennonite Air Missions since its beginning. The family has served several short terms in Guatemala.

Delilah does substitute teaching and finds the classroom to be her second home. In her busy schedule as a pastor's wife, sewing is a real relaxation.

Prompt obedience
is the only obedience God accepts.
Slow obedience
is no obedience.

Our Home

We need a special place
Where we can be set free,
To just relax and be ourselves,
To find that hidden "me."
That home we share is such a place
And I thank God above,
For giving us a happy home
So filled with His great love.
Sometimes this world is
Push and shove,
I feel so all alone
I can hardly wait 'til day is done
To reach our happy home.

—*Darlene Blackman*

Letting Go Graciously

by Anna Mary (Mrs. Bennie) Byler

O ur youngest child eagerly prepares for the first day of school. Mother watches until the big yellow school bus disappears. Tears fill her eyes and trickle down her cheeks.

Letting go? Yes. God is in supreme control, and the bus is a church school bus. So, with that confidence, Mother can turn back to her work; not fretting or worrying, but with a prayer for God's protection for that little one.

The whole family minus one watches as the plane vanishes from sight. Ahead is the foreign, unknown Belize soil.

Again letting go, and yet being confident that God is in complete control, and that mother and daughter can, through prayer, meet at God's throne.

Our only son and his dedicated Christian bride walk down the church aisle as husband and wife, hand-in-hand, facing the turbulent sea of life; yet being confident that God, Who led them together, will also keep them in His perfect will.

Yes, it hurts when a close family begins to "cut those apron strings," but this is all part of God's perfect plan for the family. Blessed are those parents who diligently prepare their children for the future and then graciously let go. (It would hurt even more to not be a close, caring family.)

What a challenge! What an awesome responsibility God gives to us.

It is my prayer that this chapter may be an encouragement to diligently teach and prepare for that "far, distant day of letting go."

Letting go is like letting a kite climb farther and farther into the distant blue while we as parents reel out the string. But there are dangers, and we still hold on until the moment arrives to hand over the controls to the divine Parent. (God gives the wisdom we need.)

We have learned to think of our home as a training center rather than a show place. Home is a laboratory where experiments are tried out. It is a place where children, especially teenagers and older, are free to think, to talk, to try out ideas and plan goals. It is the place where life makes up its mind. It is where children can be themselves and are not belittled, and where parents are open and interested in their goals and their future.

In a scene like this, God fits very comfortably into the entire conversation. At any time or place where His name is inserted, *it fits!* It is authentic (genuine, being actual and exact, not false or counterfeit)!

"When my children were yet with me" (Job 29:5) strikes a tender chord, yet we must realize our children have only been lent to us for a very short time. We must keep in mind that God has planned for us to teach them and then give them back to Him to serve in whatever way He wills.

They come to us totally *dependent* and we are called to prepare them to be relatively *independent.* Dependence would indicate to rely securely on another person. Independence is to be subject to no one, but to be self-governing. In order to nurture our children from the time they solely rely on us to the time when they are self-governing, there are some characteristics that must become part of their lives.

Children do not learn to tithe unless they are taught first by example when they are still very small. When they are given a dollar or earn a dollar, they must learn the first tenth belongs to God, and in addition to that, the Bible speaks of *offerings.*

Children will not learn on their own to be good losers. Parents must be on hand to encourage them when they are losers, that they don't give up, but try again. Also it is very important that they are cheerful losers and rejoice with the one who wins.

We must teach our children that lamenting, complaining and fretting won't make a person what he should be, but rather he must learn to joyfully accept what life holds, and to do all he can to make the most of any given situation.

It is important to teach them to always right a wrong if possible. This is being blameless as the Bible requires of Christians. If a person can't right a wrong, then he must learn a valuable lesson and not repeat the wrong. And if the wrong cannot be corrected nor used as a reminder to do better, then it must be forgotten and not allowed to keep him from "getting on with living."

What enters your mind when you hand your teenager the car keys the first time?

I remember so vividly as one by one our children came to the age when they took Driver's Ed. The final day arrived when they were handed their license by an official. There was a look of accomplishment! But with that comes the responsibility to be God-conscious rather than man-conscious when they drive. It is so important that as the parent hands over the family car keys that parent and child's eyes meet, and with that comes a commitment to be God-fearing rather than relying on the rear view mirror.

Everyday manners must be taught: for example, eating with mouth closed, praying with head bowed and eyes closed, cleaning bathtub after each use, hanging up their clothes or disposing of them in a proper way, keeping their drawers, desks, and closets orderly so they can quickly find what they are looking for. The need of courtesy doesn't just find its way into our children's lives. They must be taught to say, "Please," "Thank you," "Pardon me," "I'm sorry," and "Forgive me."

Children need to be consistently taught (but more is caught) the importance of being prompt and respectful of others' schedules and time. Also children must be taught to give and give again, rather then having the attitude of getting all they can.

Someone made the observation that a child asks between 6,000-10,000 questions from infancy to the age of 6. We must answer them honestly if we expect to have the privilege to share and answer their questions as they prepare to leave home.

Often during these years we as parents should be asking ourselves the question, "What should I be sharing with my son or daughter?" We need to especially ask God for His guidance and wisdom to better prepare them to face life.

The following are several points that may help parents who are "letting go."

   1. There will be changes. Each change will be a jarring experience.

2. We must find our happiness in God rather than in our family as it is today.
3. Our interest must be beyond ourselves and our family.
4. Encourage our children and don't make them feel guilty in growing up.
5. Keep in mind our children are only lent to us by God.

Keeping these in mind will help us to prepare properly for the transitional time when we must let go.

We as parents need to cultivate within our children a healthy respect for themselves and others so they can perform well regardless of the odds against them. We must be building determination, hope, resiliency (being pliable, elastic), and fiber into the child's inner being. That takes time! Also since we live in a real world, we need plenty of time for real communication.

Self-esteem is another ingredient that is needed if our children are to be prepared to launch out independently from parents, yet very dependent upon their heavenly Parent.

Proper self-esteem is not a noisy conceit. It is a quiet sense of self worth. With a good sense of worth, children don't need to waste precious time and energy trying to impress their peers, because they know that they are valuable to God and their parents.

If we as parents have a meaningful and heartfelt relationship with our heavenly Father, it will be one of the greatest contributions any parents can make in their children's lives.

Convictions need to be instilled deep in our children's lives. "Line upon line, precept upon precept, here a little and there a little" (Isa. 28: 10, 13). There are times when children imitate their parents' convictions; but only as our children adopt and then develop, their own convictions according to the Bible, will they be able to truly stand. If the children live only on parental conviction, they will not be able to hold forth the Word of life. That is one reason it is of utmost importance that we as parents are well grounded and that our lives are saturated by the Word of God.

Wise parents never drag their feet when their children launch out, but parents' joys increase as their children grow up.

The reward will be to see our children launch from our home, secure in Christ, confident they have been designed by God, to fulfill a special calling equipped with the tools to handle the demands of everyday life. Then by God's grace we have done our job, and God has done the rest!

"If you can guide, not push, your child along,
If you can guard, not smother, from the wrong,
If you can love, not idolize, your child,
If you can teach obedience, tame the wild
Instinctive moods, the very heart of him,
If you can pray, to save his soul from sin,
If you regard his need for elbow room,
And can remember he's an adult so soon . . .
If you can punish, and be just, as well,
If you can, too, your rising anger quell,
If you respect his personality,
Give him to God for immortality,
If you can praise, where praise is rightly due,
If you can promise, and be ever true,
If you can trust him when there is some doubt
And then can tell him when no one's about,
If you can help him through the tender years,

If you can share his secrets and his fears,
If all God's laws you train him to uphold,
Your child will not forget you when you're old."

—*Sara J. Hale*

The Zest of Life

Let me live my life from year to year,
      With forward face and unreluctant soul.
      Not hastening to, nor turning from the goal;
Not mourning for the things that disappear
In the dim past, nor holding back in fear
      From what the future holds; but with a whole
      And happy heart, that pays its toll
To youth and age, and travels on with cheer.
So let the way wind up the hill or down;
      Through rough or smooth, the journey will be joy;
      Still seeking what I sought but when a boy,
New friendship, high adventure, and a crown
      I shall grow old, but never lose life's zest,
      Because the road's last turn will be the best.

—*Henry Van Dyke*

Facing Mid-Life With Confidence

by Anna Mary (Mrs. Bennie) Byler

The mission board requested that Bennie accompany another bishop to Central America to share in Communion and baptismal services at the various mission stations. He had been exceptionally busy several weeks prior to his ten-day expedition to a foreign country. Church work required his attention, the business needed his direction, and the girls and I had questions that needed answers. Circumstances had not permitted us as husband and wife to spend much time together.

This morning as I was meditating, I knew they were taking a very small aircraft to Punta Gorda and from there, traveling in a dugout the last three hours to their destination.

The house was exceptionally quiet, the clock seemed to be ticking loudly, and the noise of the power nailers and saws drifted in through the open window. The girls had left for work and school. Although this was a typical morning, I felt frustrated.

As I opened my Bible for my private meditation, I was so blessed as I read Philippians one. I paraphrased part of verse 6: "Being confident of this very thing, that [He Who led us together will also keep us together] until the day of the Lord Jesus Christ."

247

Some of my frustration that morning had been what if . . . ? What if the Caribbean Sea was too rough to make it safely to their destination? What if that small aircraft crashed? What if . . . ?

The Lord, as always, gave the calming assurance that HE IS ABLE to calm the troubled waters and HE IS ABLE to keep the small motor running. HE IS ABLE also to "keep us together" because it was "God Who led us together," even though our lot in life had been less than the most desirable. Yes, God could also keep us together as husband and wife in the ship of marriage as we felt the waves of the turbulent sea of life.

It is possible to face life with confidence—not in our own strength, nor in the surroundings and circumstances in which we find ourselves, but as we place ALL of our confidence and trust in the great God Who changes not (Malachi 3:6).

At an evening service several years ago, a minister addressed the much-needed subject of "Growing Old Gracefully." Adult life is divided into three stages: young adulthood, mid-life, and old age. Each stage brings its care and frustrations.

With youth comes zeal to really make a mark in society. Pride is a temptation that youth faces, and peer pressure often directs their thinking. The stage of young adulthood includes vocations, marriage, babies, and preschool children. Life seemingly revolves around making a living, the husband and wife's learning to know each other, and babies becoming preschool children. Life is full and interesting. Some say, "It is the best time. Enjoy your children while they are young and innocent, while you have them in control." I do not necessarily agree! As children grow up and a good communication develops between parents and teenagers, life becomes more interesting and even more worthwhile.

At times remarks like these are heard: "I'm twenty-nine and holding;" "I never want to go 'over the hill' " (referring to age forty); or "I wish this was our wedding day again!" Seemingly, to them the thought of mid-life and growing older leaves a bad taste. A carpenter once said, "I would rather build a new house every ten years than to maintain the one we have."

Perhaps this is how we too often view middle age. This concept is all too common in society today. Unless our roots are grounded deeply and firmly in God's Word, we too may be swept away by the current. If we allow fantasy and feeling to engulf us, the "feeling" of love will dwindle. But if we by God's grace, establish in our minds God's plan for one husband and one wife, then we need not dread the changes life brings, because we cling to the unchanging promises of God.

I was challenged by what a business writer mentioned about the age forty transition. "We cannot live the afternoon of life according to the program of life's morning" (Carl Jung, *Volume Library, Book One,* Page 513). In general, it is hard, if not impossible, to change cheerfully if we have the concept that living in the glamour of youth is the best time.

No one would be satisfied to always have youthful ambitions, and to have our families stay in the preschool stage, not growing and maturing. Yet many find it difficult to accept changes cheerfully in mid-life.

Materialism is said to be the frequent goal and hindrance of middle age. It is often the time when people relax spiritually and also take each other for granted as husband and wife.

Mid-life is the time when businessmen become aware that some goals are either reached or unfulfilled. Husbands and fathers are aware that their children are growing up or even grown, and have abilities that surpass their expectations or their own management. They feel threatened. This should not be!

Psalm ninety has a lot of good admonition for those in mid-life. Verse one say GOD IS OUR DWELLING PLACE in all generations. Verses four through six remind us how fleeting time is: AS A WATCH IN THE NIGHT, AS A FLOWER THAT FLOURISHETH in the morning, and in the evening it is cut down and withers. Verse nine says our life is AS A TALE THAT IS TOLD. Verse twelve teaches us to NUMBER OUR DAYS, so we can become more godly.

If we have a proper concept of God and how short our life is, we will plead with God to SATISFY US EARLY WITH HIS MERCY, so we can rejoice and be glad ALL our days (verse 14). Yes! That includes a cheerful, changing mid-life. It is a life in which we cling to an unchanging God in the midst of a changing family, aging infirmities, and graying hair.

In verse fifteen we look to God for the gladness that He alone can give. Even in our afflictions, we will be able to see God's hand working.

Verse sixteen will be our prayer. "Let thy work appear unto thy servants, and thy glory unto their children." Our own example should assist our children to hear the quiet bidding of God, in the midst of activity. Only as we are found in Him can we ask God to let HIS BEAUTY BE SEEN, and He will establish the work of our hands, that even in old age His beauty can be displayed in the lives of those who have learned to grow old gracefully.

If our lives are filled with God in our youth and

continued on into mid-life, then in old age Satan will not be able to plague us with doubt and defeat because it is God's perfect plan to BRING FORTH FRUIT IN OLD AGE (Psalm 92:14).

A wise minister once said that if he had known at the age of twenty what he knows at the age of fifty-eight, he would have taken life much more seriously. Yet many go on their own way, giving little attention to history, or the experience and conviction of older and more mature people. Of course, they reap what they sow (Galatians 6:7). God never intended that every generation should make the same mistakes.

A model marriage, one that is to stand the test of time, is said to be founded in pure, godly love and cemented in mutual esteem. Then we will approach God at His throne hand in hand. No bitterness can prevail in our hearts if we approach the Light of Infinite Love and confess our sins. Seeking Him together and sharing the same goals gives faith and inspiration, and promises immortality to the love we share.

When young couples see those in middle age whose love and respect for each other is still growing, it is encouraging. So also when we see those grandparents who are faithful, it gives hope and security that God's plan is the best.

As husbands and wives we must continue to be convinced that marriage is for life, and the commitment we made on our wedding day is still as binding as it was then: ". . . for better or worse, in joy or sorrow, to love and cherish, in prosperity and adversity, live in peace, forsaking all others, as long as we both live."

Communication is a blessed virtue. "If the Son therefore shall make you free, you shall be free indeed" (John

8:36). We are free to think, free to create, free to share openly, free to be all God intended us to be, free to become more godly and to grow in Christ. Then we are useful in life, and we will rejoice in eternity.

A great deal of inward unrest comes from basing peace of mind on our surroundings. However, great spiritual riches await all Christians who grow older gracefully.

Old age brings decay and disillusionment to the body, but to the person who lives for God and lives in His Spirit, there will be triumph.

The denial of age and death are partially responsible for people living empty, purposeless lives. When a person lives with little concept of time, it becomes easy to procrastinate and put off what must be done. By contrast, when we are aware that today may be our last day, we take time to allow God to give us spiritual growth to become more Christlike, and to live for the good of others.

In order to have a meaningful goal in mid-life and as we grow older, we must look deeply into life, and we will see continuity in all our years of serving God.

He is the happiest person who can reconcile the end of his life with its beginning. As we grow older we can see that the greatest successes have been times of obedience to our Heavenly Father.

The things which do the most
to make us happy,
do not cost money.

IF . . .

If a child lives with criticism, he learns to condemn.

If a child lives with hostility, he learns to fight.

If a child lives with fears, he learns to be
apprehensive.

If a child lives with pity, he learns to feel sorry for
himself.

If a child lives with jealousy, he learns to feel guilty.

If a child lives with encouragement, he learns to be
confident.

If a child lives with tolerance, he learns to be
patient.

If a child lives with praise, he learns to be
appreciative.

If a child lives with acceptance, he learns to love.

If a child lives with approval, he learns to like
himself.

If a child lives with recognition, he learns to have a
goal.

If a child lives with fairness, he learns what justice
is.

If a child lives with honesty, he learns what truth is.

If a child lives with security, he learns to have faith in
himself and in those about him.

If a child lives with friendliness, he learns that the
world is a good place in which to live.

—*The Watchman-Examiner*

The Far-Reaching Effect of Faithful Children

by Anna Mary (Mrs. Bennie) Byler

C enturies ago there was a godly woman whose character has been a good example to follow. Hannah, the Bible tells us, was loved by her husband, Elkanah, but she had no children; and this brought sorrow to her life.

According to the customs, each year Elkanah and his two wives and their children went to the temple to worship and sacrifice unto the Lord.

While Hannah was there, she vowed a vow and said "O Lord of hosts, if thou wilt indeed look on the affliction of thine handmaid and remember me and not forget thine handmaid, but wilt give unto thine handmaid a man child, then I will give him unto the Lord *all* the days of his life . . ." (I Sam. 1:11).

God answered her prayer, and in due time Samuel was born. His name means, "because I have asked him of the Lord."

Hannah did not go to the temple yearly until Samuel was weaned (I Sam. 1:22-24). Then she took Samuel to the temple and said to Eli, "Oh my lord, as thy soul liveth my lord, I am the woman that stood by thee here, praying unto the Lord. For this child I prayed; and the Lord hath given me my petition which I asked of him; therefore also I lent him to the Lord; as long as he liveth he shall be lent to the Lord" (vv. 26-28). Giving this child to the Lord was the joy of her life!

The second chapter of I Samuel is headlined, "Hannah's thanksgiving." Gratitude is a very important aspect in the life of one who has dedicated her child or children to the Lord before they are born.

Hannah is a good example of a mother who is a reflection of God to her child. Her very life spoke of God. The first step, was her obedience in complying with the yearly worship and sacrifices at the temple, even though she had no children. She came alone.

God honored her obedience as a young woman and her faith in God. The story tells us she poured her anguish out before God, even to the extent that Eli thought she was drunk. It seems her life depended on God's answer, and truly it did!

Another example that we can draw from Hannah is she lived a consistent life, and the outstanding fact is she not only prayed but made a vow. She meant every word she uttered. God richly blessed her consistent life, and the important fact is that she lived what she prayed. Not once does the Bible indicate any reluctance, but when she took Samuel back to the temple, thanksgiving followed. What a challenging example of unselfishness!

As we study the life of Samuel we note the far-reaching effect his life had on the people of God. "The Lord was with him, and did let none of his words fall to the ground" (I Sam. 3:19).

Webster defines discipline as dedication, the mental grasping for a desired goal. It is defined as training which corrects, molds, strengthens, and perfects. To be a dedicated mother requires discipline. For deeper dedication we need to love correction and desire to be strengthened, molded more in our Saviour's likeness. If we desire for our children to be dedicated, we need to discipline our lives so God can perfect us.

James M. Hitch says, "Training is the process by which the behavior of one person is changed into conformity with the standard exemplified by another. Or in other words, it is the process in which one person takes another person in his behavior, to the place where the first person already is" (God's Pattern for Enriched Living).

It is essential to be practicing what you want your children to practice. The best way to teach character is to be living examples of it in the home.

God's method of teaching us in the way of total dedication is a positive approach and so our training must also be positive.

We differentiate between threatening and giving warnings. *Threatening* is the repetition of promised correction, without a follow-through of promised action. *Warning* is spoken once and the follow-through is certain! Warning constitutes a very important part of effective discipline.

Many discipline problems can be eliminated by being consistent!

When we ask a child *why* he did a certain wrong we are encouraging him to rationalize the wrong and excuse himself. When he faces the question, "What did you do?" he learns to admit his wrong. This will also train him to properly respond to God. God is not interested in *why* we did a certain thing, but *what* we did. He simply asks us to confess our sins.

Neither is the judge interested in why we violated the law. He simply wants to know whether we plead guilty or not guilty regarding the charge.

Remember, we dare not attempt to control the child's total will, but to break his self-will.

Breaking and conquering the child's self-will through the proper measure of discipline, frees the child to become a God-pleaser. This, of course, should be the ultimate concern of the parents so our children will become God-conscious and therefore allow God to control their whole being.

The Bible relates another interesting account of one whose dedication was outstanding, and a model down through the ages. It is interesting to note that Esther was an orphan. Her cousin Mordecai opened his heart and home to one in need. All through the book of Esther her dedication stands out, as does also the dedication of Mordecai.

In the book of Esther, as in the story of Hannah, obedience precedes dedication. Esther was a young girl who had a high respect for her "adopted father," and throughout the book we see her deep desire to obey Mordecai. Through her unselfish life, her obedience and dedication, God brought deliverance to His people, the Jews. Esther reserved nothing for herself.

Mordecai admonished Esther, "Think not with thyself that thou shalt escape in the king's house, more than all the Jews. . . . and who knoweth whether thou art come to the kingdom for such a time as this" (4:13, 14).

Verse 16 shows Esther's total dedication to God and His work. Her response to Mordecai was, "If I perish, I perish." In the example of Esther, it is her disciplined life that stands out. Discipline brings dedication.

The last verse in the book of Esther tells again of the far-reaching effect of faithful children, those who are willing to totally give everything to the Lordship of Christ.

Mordecai was "seeking the wealth of his people and speaking peace to all his seed."

Timothy is another example of a life of dedication. His life reached far into the early churches. Paul spoke of being "filled with joy; when I call to remembrance the unfeigned faith that is in *thee,* which dwelt first in thy grandmother Lois and thy mother Eunice; and I am convinced that in thee also" (2 Tim. 1:4c, 5).

Years ago, in observing people, I noticed one elderly couple that stood out to me as having had the wisdom of child training. Their family was grown and most of their children were missionaries and ministers of the gospel, zealous in the Lord's work. One day I was privileged to ask the wife and mother the important question. "What is the secret in bringing children to the Lord?" She answered, after a few minutes of thought, "I think the downfall of the home is not enough Loises and Eunices: mothers and grandmothers of unfeigned faith, prayer and love."

All of us want our children to be such as God can use in touching people's lives for the Lord. So the question and challenges come back to us as grandmothers and mothers, "Are we willing to dedicate our whole lives, so that our children and grandchildren can be effective for God?"

"Mark well her bulwarks, consider her palaces that ye may tell it to generations following. For this God is our God for ever and ever: he will be our guide even unto death" (Ps. 48:13, 14).

Bulwarks could be our home as we consider God being our God forever and ever, and our guide unto death. We need to mark well (or hold in apreciation) our families. Appreciate our palaces or homes so we can pass the blessing on to the generations that follow. Bulwark means a solid wall of defense, strong protection. That is what our homes and families should be!

The need to strengthen our marriage is all important if we want our children to be dedicated and to carry on God's purpose for their lives.

"Enlarge the place of thy tent, and let them stretch forth the curtains of thine habitations: spare not, lengthen thy cords, and strengthen thy stakes" (Isa. 54:2).

If we as parents truly have a vision of God's standard for our tents or homes, we will be willing to enlarge the love of the family, appreciate and encourage each family member. Dad and Mom will have a godly respect for each other and therefore, will be available to help their children "stretch" or broaden their capacity in God's work. We as parents will also be willing to give encouragement, admonition and corrections as needed, always bathed with love and prayer. We will help our families to deepen their commitment to God and the church, and will strengthen the convictions of those around them.

Then and then only can we claim the blessed promise, "All thy children shall be taught of the Lord; and great shall be the peace of thy children" (Isa. 54:13). What encouragement, what a challenge to be our best for God.

Then there is also a very sad picture in Jeremiah 10:20: "My tabernacle is spoiled, and all my cords are broken: my children are gone forth from me, and they are not: there is none to stretch my tent any more, and to set up my curtains."

Let's notice the contrast. Isaiah 54:1 mentions enlarging. This means growth or expansion. The tabernacle or home that is at a standstill is on the way to destruction. We need to continually enlarge or expand or grow in God's way. Isaiah suggests that we families, and especially parents, teach or "stretch" our children's capacity of obedience and discipline to further the work of God. We are to teach by example, by pattern, precept upon precept, line upon line, and therefore lengthen the strong cords that are anchors for the home.

In Jeremiah 10:20 the cords are broken: relationships, togetherness, and love that bind the family together are broken. Children that are left to themselves will have no conviction that would build or that would withstand the trials of life.

Again, God's word has the answer in verse 21: "For the pastors [parents] are become brutish, and have not sought the Lord: therefore they shall not prosper, and all their flocks [children] shall be scattered." Webster defines brutish as strongly and grossly sensual, shows little intelligence or sensibility, lack of understanding. What a sad picture, but as always, God does not leave us to find our own way through a troublesome situation. Verses 23 and 24 again give us the answer if there is a willingness for true repentance and a total dedication to God. "O Lord, I know that the way of man is not in himself: it is not in man that walketh to direct his step, O Lord, correct me, but with judgment and not in thine anger, lest thou bring me to nothing."

There are always some practical things that God would have us consider and make a part of our life and home if we sincerely desire our children to become channels through which God's work can go on and have a far-reaching effect on the on-coming generations.

Ten points to consider as the key to keep the respect and confidence of our children are:

1. Be honest and open, answer questions honestly.
2. Admit when we fail, submit to those in authority over us.

3. Love, forgive; when a child is once punished, don't bring the issue up again.
4. Be consistent, firm, balanced. Children want to know limits.
5. Acknowledge when we are wrong and ask forgiveness.
6. Be totally impartial!
7. Spend time daily in Bible reading and prayer. Bind God's Word into your heart and your total life.
8. Be dedicated to God's Word and work.
9. Be a good listener. Use all five senses.
10. Know what is going on. (Cultivate that togetherness while young children play when mother works!)

I trust all of us have goals for our children, but more importantly for our own lives.

At a recent Parent-Teacher Fellowship, a short and challenging topic on goals was presented. The question was asked what goals do you have for your children? This is a fair question to ask ourselves occasionally.

Since I was meditating on this question, I was made aware that some of our goals have been fulfilled by our children and what greater joy is there in parents than to see "our children walking in the truth" (III John 4)?

Our goal as a young married couple had been to serve a term in Central America, but God said, "No, take care of your widowed mother." So Bennie's mother lived with us the first six years of our married life. Later our oldest daughter sensed the call and served two years as school teacher in Belize.

I always enjoyed studying and would have been delighted to further my education, but our church setting would not have permitted it. Instead, we got married at a young age. Now, two of our children were privileged to take high school courses and the third one anticipates high school.

I loved music and singing, yet it never was my lot to pursue these interests. Now God has blessed us with a son who has dedicated much time and effort in teaching music and the meaning of the words and songs we sing.

Another one of our daughters is teaching school, a very worthy vocation. Although I was not able to teach, this goal has been reached by God calling our daughter to teach. Yes, I am able to encourage her and help her with the bulletin boards and charts, cleaning and checking papers and books. Now I feel my goals are being fulfilled through our children.

I am aware, however, that while it is right to experience a sense of fulfillment in this, children should be allowed to develop as persons in their own rights, not merely an extension of the unfulfilled goals of parents.

Let us do as David said, " I have set the Lord always before me; because he is at my right hand, I shall not be moved" (Ps. 16:8). If our focus is set on God we will have similar goals for our children. Seeing them being fulfilled, by God's grace, we rejoice in the far-reaching effect of faithful children.

" . . . I count not myself
to have *achieved;*
but this one thing I do . . .
reaching forth to those things
which are before.
I press toward the mark
of the high calling
of Jesus Christ."

Philippians 3: 13-14

Notes

TO ORDER

For additional copies send $6^{99}
(plus 2^{00} postage and handling)
to:
The Bylers
Rt. 1 Box 630
Stuarts Draft, Virginia 24477

Quantity discounts available.

Name _____

Address _____

City _____ State_____ Zip_____

Quantity ordered_____

Amount enclosed_____

Virginia residents please include 4.5% sales tax

TO ORDER

For additional copies send $6^{99}
(plus 2^{00} postage and handling)
to:
The Bylers
Rt. 1 Box 630
Stuarts Draft, Virginia 24477

Quantity discounts available.

Name _____ .

Address _____

City _____ State_____ Zip_____

Quantity ordered_____

Amount enclosed_____

Virginia residents please include 4.5% sales tax